Web of Silence

Web of Silence

Letters to Meditators

LAURENCE FREEMAN

DARTON·LONGMAN + TODD

Published in association with Medio Media

To Bal, Linda and Bethany
with love and gratitude

First published in 1996 by
Darton, Longman and Todd Ltd
1 Spencer Court
140–142 Wandsworth High Street
London SW18 4JJ

ISBN 0–232–52171–9

A catalogue record for this book is available
from the British Library

Bible quotations are taken from the New English Bible, copyright © 1970
Cambridge University Press, and the New Jerusalem Bible, published and
copyright © 1967, 1968 and 1969 by Darton, Longman and Todd Ltd and
Doubleday and Co. Inc.

Phototypeset in 8½/12½pt Leawood Book by Intype London Ltd
Printed and bound in Great Britain by
Page Bros, Norwich

Contents

Introduction

These letters were written to friends, meditators around the world within the Christian Meditation Community, many of whom I have never met. Meditation has a mysterious power of opening friendship between people at a level deeper than we are usually familiar with. The normal social barriers and suspicions seem to dismantle very quickly when you have sat in silence with someone. Courtesy replaces formal politeness. Trust replaces social distance. This humanising quality of meditation is even further enhanced between people who know that they are sharing a common spiritual path, a twice-daily practice of silence as we teach it in our Community. Any discipline requires support, encouragement and ongoing inspiration. Even when we believe strongly in something and enjoy it, there are times when we get discouraged or run into dryness, impatience or doubt. Because of this meditation fosters community. These letters were written to help that process.

The World Community for Christian Meditation is a personal network of people of all ages and backgrounds, and of many types of faith, who are friends because they meditate. When we have international gatherings, at retreats or at the annual John Main Seminar, for example, it is one of the most delightful experiences to meet people for the first time and feel within a few minutes that you are close to each other at a level that really matters. These meetings are not forgotten.

The Community is made up of a worldwide web of individual meditators who follow the Christian tradition of silent, nondiscursive meditation which John Main recovered from the early Christian monastic wisdom and passed on to the late twentieth-century church. Bede Griffiths once remarked that John Main's two greatest contributions to this church were his recovery of a method of contemplative prayer that could be practised by people in any walk of life and the insight that meditation creates community. These individual meditators are the beneficiaries of these fruits of John Main's own spiritual pilgrimage and his prophetic courage.

Individuals cluster into groups in all fields of life. In the meditation field small weekly groups are flourishing around the world. This is a phenomenon, silent but deeply hopeful, which deserves more attention than the media usually give it. Meditation networks of many kinds and many faiths, Buddhist and Christian in particular, explore the spiritual depths of their own traditions and are open in tolerance and co-operation to each other's. The quality of life and awareness which these communities nurture point towards a saner, healthier, more humane world.

In our Christian Meditation Community weekly groups meet in parishes, homes, prisons, offices, schools and hospitals. Each group follows a simple, threefold format: a teaching (often a tape by John Main), a period of meditation in silence for thirty minutes and a time then for discussion or questions. These groups are often composed of only a few regular meditators. But this core group becomes a living community of faith: a contemplative community. Schools of deep prayer, they teach newcomers and they encourage the experienced to persevere.

Meditation groups of this kind rise and fall and, like everything in our hurtling world today, they are subject to change and insecurity. Sometimes the most fragile groups emit the strongest waves of faith and touch lives in the most decisive ways. It always strikes me as a remarkable aspect of these groups that they are centres of stability for our world. And they are points of light, small and steady rather than bright and brief, in a world so often only conscious of its own darkness.

There is a certain paradox in meditation creating community or in having anything like an international organisation for meditation. It sounds a bit like a conference of hermits. Meditation, it is true, is a path of solitude. Solitude is, however, not essentially about physical withdrawal and certainly it is not about emotional isolation. Real solitude is the reverse of loneliness and alienation. It is the encounter and embracing of our uniqueness – something we find rather terrifying at first. Once we have tasted solitude, however, we see the fruits of it in an enhanced gift for empathy and compassion, for sincere communication and so for community. It is not just because John Main was a Benedictine monk that the Christian Meditation Community can be described in this 'monastic' language or that the developing worldwide community finds in the Rule of St Benedict and the teachings of the early Christian monks of the desert an inspiration for its life and development. It is because the experience of meditation itself contacts and uncovers the monk in each person.

By monk I mean St Benedict's basic definition – one who truly seeks God. We seek God not because of where we live or what we wear or even what we do in our working hours. Seeking God is the combination of stillness, silence and simplicity in the midst of a life of noise, activity and complexity. Anyone who tries this search even once will soon discover the meaning and value of the monastic precepts of discipline, harmony of life (body, mind and spirit), obedience as selfless attention, compassion and the sharing of time and space with each other.

The Community of meditators, groups and Centres which has grown up from the grassroots since John Main's pioneering work began in 1975 has developed a form or structure by stages. The International Centre in London and its publishing company, Medio Media, serve this Community with the twenty-five other local Centres and many meditation groups. Retreats and seminars, books, tapes and videos, visits and tours are among the work of the Community – as well as 'the newsletter'. Every quarter a letter goes to meditators around the world. As far as finances permit, everyone who wants to receive a copy will be sent one. There is a suggested offering but not a formal subscription. The letter is copied and distributed by national Centres. Sometimes when the Centres see their end of year bank balance they look – who doesn't today? – at ways of cutting costs. The newsletter list is often a prime target. I try to persuade them to leave people on the list even if they haven't heard from them for a while. I argue this strongly for the same reason that I keep writing these letters after thirteen years.

Time and again on my travels I meet people who tell me that the newsletter – both the spiritual letter and the news – has arrived at crucial moments in their journey. It encouraged them to start again or to persevere. It addressed a question that had been disturbing them. Or a small story or news item delighted, amused or inspired them in a way that made them feel that their solitude was actually a relationship with an invisible but strongly present community of spiritual friends.

A few years ago I was giving talks in Barbados. At a church one afternoon I was struck by a very attentive, humbly dressed woman in the front row. She came to speak to me afterwards and the impression of a very awake and spiritually alive woman was confirmed. She was a simple woman and lived in poverty near the church. She had joined the meditation group started by the parish priest and, she told me, enjoyed the newsletter. When it arrived she would sit on her porch in her rocking chair and read it carefully and slowly. I have rarely been more encouraged to meet the deadline of the quarterly letter than by the picture of that woman's quiet, steady single-mindedness.

Of course people do say too that they cannot get round to reading the newsletter. There are so many other brown envelopes flopping through the letterbox. It is too long. There should be more short news items, less intellectual content, and so on. In writing the letters I am always influenced by the positive and negative comments and each letter tries to adapt in some way to a different kind of person or need. But these newsletters belong to a kind that does demand a certain dedication of time and attention. That is perhaps one good reason for publishing them as a book.

My own inspiration for writing these letters each quarter comes from the Community of meditators as well as from the light cast by meditation itself on the small and ordinary activities and concerns of daily life. I hope they will be an opportunity for their new readers to reflect on the wonder of life lived in Christian faith. And no small part of that wonder is that it awakens a sense of our deep unity with people of other faiths and traditions as well as with those brave souls who make their journey alone without labels of any kind.

One cannot contribute to the avalanche of published material, in quarterly letters or in books, without wondering whether it is worth while or even justifiable. My defence would be to say that in these letters I am putting in a word for silence. As the world moves so rapidly into ever denser folds of communication its need for silence grows proportionately. The Internet has exploded into modern consciousness with exciting vistas of communication and conversation opening up across cultures and time-zones. The terrible risk is that it will produce nothing but more noise in the head; and if we hear only noise we turn off and cease to communicate altogether.

The 'law of white spaces' is an important piece of universal legislation that we ignore at our personal and collective peril. The law states that it is the white space between the words on a page that make it readable. Or the silence between two musical notes. Or the rest between periods of action. Without periods of silence and non-action our words and our deeds jumble up into meaningless spirals of stress. We need a web of silence spread around the world just as extensively as the web of technology.

In fact, as the developing networks of spiritual groups around the world testify, such a web of silence already exists. This web of silence will become ever more personal, deeply personal and must therefore form itself into community. As a community it will be an active working symbol of the underlying unity of humanity in a world of diverse faiths and cultures. Meditation, the universal human spiritual tradition, is both the way of silence and the way of deep community, communion with ourselves and others, with the terrestrial environment, with the universe and with God.

These letters respond to the experience of community which Christian meditation has brought forth, and they try to nourish it. The Christian Meditation Newsletter began with John Main's first letter in 1977. Since then each letter contains both news of the Community – information about retreats and other events, new groups or Centres, publications or conferences – and a letter which reflects at some length on a spiritual topic. This spiritual part of the letter is a small part of an ongoing project, emerging out of the silence of meditation itself, to help to renew the language in which the gospel can be communicated.

It is important to nurture our sense of the link between communion, communication and community. They are three of the most intense concerns of modern culture. This book tries to do so, firstly, by referring back to the silence from which it emerges and to which it hopes it may lead its readers more deeply. Then, in including the chronicle of the Community's news over the period in which the letters were written, I hope to suggest that the 'spiritual' side of the letter is by no means abstract or ungrounded. And, finally, these letters have also been collected and published in order to help our Community to share itself and its growing experience of the Spirit more widely with the larger community of which we are a part.

I am very grateful to Gregory Ryan, the regional co-ordinator of the Community in New Jersey, who put so much into the preparation of these letters for publication. Dom Placid Meylink, the prior, and my Benedictine community of the Monastery of Christ the King, Cockfosters, also richly deserve both my thanks and that of the World Community for Christian Meditation for their warm and generous affirmation of the work which these letters point to, and for freeing me to serve it. My community at the London Christian Meditation Centre, Eileen, Elizabeth,

Giovanni and Ria do not need to be told that they contribute richly to the content and writing of these letters as well as to their production and mailing. The team at the International Centre, Teresa, Michael, Sadie, Susan, Dorcas and Judith, and the extended web of meditators who share the work of silence worldwide are also very much part of whatever these letters may do as they step out in their new attire.

Laurence Freeman OSB
International Centre,
The World Community for Christian Meditation
London
January 1996

Letter One

February 1992

Dearest Friends,

As you enter the great thirteenth-century cathedral of Chartres through the west door you find yourself walking onto and into the Pilgrims' Labyrinth. The labyrinth is drawn in black stone on the floor of the nave of the cathedral under the rose window, whose diameter it reflects exactly. During the Middle Ages poor pilgrims, who were unable to go to Jerusalem, would make a symbolic 'pilgrimage' on their knees around all the twists and turns of the labyrinth in their own cathedral.

In Chartres, as in many European cathedrals, where similar designs were once to be found, this spiritual mandala acquired great meaning in the devotion of the laity. Many generations experienced the joy of arriving at the centre of the labyrinth after many doubts and hesitations. During the Age of Reason, however, most of these labyrinths came to be seen as foolish superstitions and were removed. During the French Revolution, in fact, Chartres Cathedral, dedicated to our Lady, was rededicated to the 'Goddess Reason', but the labyrinth happily survived. Today, however, on entering the church you find the labyrinth covered and hidden by chairs.

I was in Chartres recently. As I walked the stone design of the labyrinth it struck me how powerful and helpful a symbol of the inner journey it is; and how its history and present condition is symbolic of the contemplative tradition at the heart of the Christian faith. If you trace the labyrinth, here reproduced, with your finger you will begin to understand why John Main

considered meditation not merely a method of prayer but a
pilgrimage and a way of life. Making the pilgrimage of the labyrinth with devotion, like meditation, illuminates the journey of
our life. All the loops and backtracks of the labyrinth help to
put our times of dryness and peace (what the early monks called
acedia and *apatheia*) in the perspective of the overall design of
the journey.

We begin at the beginning. Every human journey, even a
spiritual one which transcends time and space, has a definite
beginning. We are not far from the centre of the labyrinth even
at the beginning, but we have a journey to make, a process of
realisation and self-discovery, before we can find ourselves to
be in fact already and always at the centre. At the outset it
seems we will get to the centre on a straight run, but we soon
encounter the recurrent patterns of loops and bends that test
and deepen our faith. They can make it seem we are losing
ground, turning back; and after years of meditation we can

think we have made no progress – except in the maturing of our faith, which is the essential meaning of spiritual growth. This same faith then shows us that the twists and turns of the journey are not God's way of making life more difficult, but a compassionate and wise teacher's way of untying the knots of our heart.

The labyrinth shows us the wisdom of not trying to measure our progress, precisely because the journey is not linear and mental but cyclical and spiritual, like the coils of a spring. All that matters is the confidence of knowing that we are on the way. The path to the centre is a narrow one, but it leads to the source of life which is eternal. We have only to stay on the path. If we try to cheat and jump over from where we are to where we want to be without going the way we must go, we get lost and confused. But at any point we can start again. The ever-present compassion of God is experienced most directly in the constancy of the way and in the ultimate discovery, at the centre, of the meaning of the journey we have made. We have only to keep moving forward in faith, for whoever seeks will find.

Meditation is a way. It is first of all a way of experience rather than of thought or imagination. Even a symbol such as the labyrinth points to this. A symbol such as the Pilgrims' Labyrinth of Chartres, though rich in meaning, is only truly understood when it is seen to point beyond itself and out of the world of signs altogether. Looking at an illustration of the labyrinth and tracing the journey to the centre with your finger is very different from doing it in reality on your knees. How different then is the daily practice of meditation from merely reading or talking about it. In meditation we move deeper than the experience of the experience. We realise that our true centre is not in the ego. This lets us go deeper, beyond self-conscious experience to a new level and clarity in the experience of God, where we are no longer projecting onto God but letting go of God, letting God be. To do this we have simply to go beyond thought altogether. Every thought of God, said St Gregory of Nyssa, is an idol.

The redemptive experience lies at the heart of every Christian life. It is redemption from the mind's palace of mirrors and the ego's prison of self-centredness. And it is redemption for an unbounded openness to that fullness of being which is a sharing in the love at the true centre of our selves and of the universe. It is this spiritual, not mental or psychological, knowledge of love that redeems us.

Experience demands faith, and meditation is also a way of faith. The poor pilgrims of Chartres, down through the centuries, had not mastered understanding of the dogma of Christian belief but it was to the faith of such as them that God revealed the Mystery. Jesus 'exulted in the Holy Spirit' when he thanked his Father for revealing these things to the simple (Luke 10:21). In meditation we go deeper than beliefs and all external signs into the heart of faith. Here we understand how faith is a gift of God because it is that point in ourselves where we can open to the reality beyond the rational mind. Here too we discover that we can experience all that Jesus experienced when he said 'I know where I come from and I know where I am going. The Father and I are one.' Through our union with him, 'in faith', deeper than belief, we are no longer once removed from God but brought close. If we relate to Jesus only through the mind and belief we can never follow him totally. He remains a histori-cal person from whom we will always be separate. Through faith, in the heart and beyond the mind, we meet him in the unity of love which is the Spirit. In love the experience of the one becomes that of the other.

The early English mystics spoke of prayer as the way of 'oneing'. What makes us whole, or 'one', is healing; meditation is therefore also a way of healing. Jesus taught that faith makes us whole. The sick need to have faith in the cure in order to overcome what can often be a deep fear of the medicine. Above all, we must have the courage to be healed of the wounds left by our unmet needs. We must face these wounds, pass through them and acknowledge our needs in poverty of spirit. This is most effectively done through deep inner stillness. 'The specific characteristic of a person at rest is to sit,' said St Gregory the Great. Silence is the root meaning of the word *hesychia* which is the Eastern Christian word for the prayer of the heart. In stillness, the healing power of the One who unites all in love rises from the deep centre of our being.

When he met the needs of the hungry crowd of five thousand Jesus had them sit down in small groups of fifty. Healing takes place in community, not in crowds; and more faith is needed to live in the love of community than in the egotistical suffering of crowds. The miracle of the feeding of the crowd is that community was created when people had enough faith to share their needs and to share what little they had. Then the abundance of God was released and there was more than enough.

The same occurs when we meditate. Whether alone or in a group we always meditate in community. We acknowledge and share our needs. We do so in stillness, in the faith Jesus taught, that the Father knows our needs before we ask him. And from the centre which is the one and eternal centre there arises, in and through each wounded heart, the abundant love that is the source equally of creation and redemption.

As this healing of the wounds of lovelessness takes place in us we realise how meditation is also a way of joy. There can, of course, be suffering in healing as well as in wounding, but joy is unquenched by any type of suffering when suffering is 'accepted in God's way'. St Paul says the suffering that remains egocentric leads to death: bitterness, paralysis of feeling and the venom of hatred and revenge. But the suffering accepted from the true centre of the person is transformed into sacrifice and releases the joy of being. The sacrifice at the heart of all love is the laying down of the ego for the other; at the moment of apparent extinction the spring of eternal life is unlocked and a transformation of reality, an awakening into reality, takes place. We get an overview of the labyrinth that is joy, *ecstasis*. All authentic human joys are epiphanies of this essential joy of arriving at the centre of the labyrinth of creation and of consciousness. None of these epiphanies of joy are to be despised because through each, however fleetingly, we glimpse where we always, really and truly are even while we are journeying to the centre.

Joy is never authentic while it is mingled with a sense of triumph or of achievement. These betray the traces of egotism which can hold us back from the fullness of being. Joy is simple when it arises within the experience of finding. To find the centre is only to realise or to discover that any true centre is also the one eternal centre. The contemplative life means only to live from this centre in every thought and deed of every day. We live and move and have our being in God. The way to the centre of the labyrinth is the teacher himself: the one who authentically says 'I am the Way'. As we discover that this joy of God is the natural fruit of meditation we also see how shortsighted, and what an egotistical perspective it betrays, to look for the results of our efforts in meditation as if they were rewards. The fruits of meditation are not the rewards for our efforts, but the natural growth of being and doing what God means us to be and do.

The New Testament naturally associates peace and joy as expressions of a life centred in Christ. As is the danger with all vocabularies, these words have often become mere Christian jargon. We talk of peace, love and joy and the fruits of the spirit because they are things that should characterise our life together, rarely because they actually do. Nor can they, unless the journey to the centre has passed from the external to the interior. Meditation is also a way of peace because it pushes us forward, or deeper, into that inner centre of the heart where all the illusions, pretence and self-deception that block us from peace are dissolved. Because we so often rationalise our desires and prejudices we need a way such as meditation that takes us to a perception deeper than reason. Meditation is best practised not as a way of achieving understanding but as a way of shedding ignorance, removing the veil that pretends to separate us from the glory which is our true identity. In losing ignorance we discover the inherent harmony of things and that they are interconnected at deeper and deeper levels. Because everything is in relationship, everything is subject to change, but change does not destroy the harmony of being which is in perpetual balance. Change reveals harmony when we stand still before it in faith.

We will never find peace in the midst of our worries and problems by thinking our way through them. Thought is a false labyrinth that always returns us to the same confused starting-point. Prayer is the true labyrinth that takes us deeper than thought and leads us to the peace that 'passes all understanding'. Letting go of our anxieties is our greatest difficulty, which testifies to the negative resilience of the ego. Yet it is so simple. We have only to grasp the true nature of meditation: not that we are trying to think of nothing, but that we are not thinking.

This is why Fr John preferred to talk of meditation as a way of attention rather than concentration. Concentration requires effort while attention is simple and natural. We concentrate on a problem. We give our attention to a thing of beauty. Meditation does not mean thinking of only one thing, as when we concentrate on an idea or problem at the mental level. It means rather stepping outside all the thinking which obstructs our full awareness of our union with the centre. The journey of meditation is coming to full attention, and it is only made with the grace of God. God inspires both the will and the deed for his own chosen purpose (Philippians 2:13). God pushes from the outside and pulls from the inside of the labyrinth. In this tension of God's grace we find the peace of the divine reality. We simply enjoy the truth. Aquinas knew this when he said that contemplation is simple enjoyment of the truth.

On my recent visit to Asia I was wonderfully inspired by the deepening and the expansion of the meditators I met with there. It was also enlightening to see the quick and welcome response made by groups newly introduced to meditation. This was true among seminarians and religious with whom retreats were held in India but also, and especially, among students and laypeople of all ages. I particularly remember a sunny morning spent with a group of students between the ages of sixteen and twenty-two. Their attention and their seriousness about prayer impressed us all and we hope that the meditation group some of them plan to start at St Teresa's girls' school in Ernakulam will flourish.

In the Philippines there has been a real growth both in depth and in the numbers of groups. The centre in Manila is expressing this by hosting a conference for Asian meditators in November to reflect on the future of contemplative Christianity in the East. In Singapore, where the first Asian groups started five years ago, I met with group leaders and with meditators who were coming to the end of a series of introductory talks and who were about to go on to join existing groups or start new ones.

The experience of others shows us that the journey is both interior and external. It is hidden and yet it has many manifestations. It is silent and yet it leads to people meeting and sharing their journey. Inasmuch as there come structures and organisation to support the visible forms of the Community which meditation calls into being, there will inevitably be frictions and irritations; even deep disappointments. But these forms should not be confused with the essence of the experience of communion, joy and peace. As people come closer to each other the ego seems to get stronger, more threatened by the communion in which it will eventually disappear. But this is no reason to draw back. It is every reason to go deeper. And indeed the inspiration we can all feel in seeing the growth of this contemplative way around the world should energise us to go deeper into the silence and stillness from which it comes and in which it must remain rooted if it is to grow and fulfil its mission. In the deepest sense we can imagine, much deeper than anything we can say or even feel, we share the experience of the labyrinth with each other.

Apart from the faithful individual meditator, the meditation group is the best communal sign of this journey that unites us all. It is a real contemporary school of faith, open to any true seeker. It unites the most interior of experiences to ordinary life, as in the meditation group recently started in a department store in Manila. It introduces beginners and encourages the more experienced with the reminder that we are always beginning. The size of a group is quite unimportant. An unnoticed group of two may by its faith be adding more to the invisible fund of wisdom that redeems the world than a 'successful' group of twenty. Indeed, as a deeper faith is probably needed to sustain a small group, we might almost say: the smaller the better. Here we touch the paradoxical wisdom of the Beatitudes in which materialistic and egotistic values are reversed. It is the lesson which the church has constantly to relearn.

In many ancient labyrinths it was a monster that was found at the centre, a thing of fear and a threat to life. The Christian labyrinths positioned Christ at the centre of all the twists and turns of life. In Christ we find not fear but the dissolving of fear in the final and primal certainty of love. Meditation is the work of love and it is by love, not by thought, that God ultimately is known: the knowledge that saves is the knowledge of love. This is why Fr John describes our human experience of love as the best way to understand why we meditate and how meditation takes us into reality. As in any relationship we pass through stages. At each stage of growth there will always be a crisis, another leap of faith. We all pass through cycles: enthusiasm, struggle with discipline, dryness and temporary enlightenments. But as fellow pilgrims we remind each other from within the labyrinth that the centre is our true home, where we are just ourselves. And we remember that there would be no flashes of joy, no temporary awakenings, if joy were not the nature of reality and if Christ had not awakened to it once and for all and in love for us all.

With much love

Laurence

Laurence Freeman OSB

Letter Two

The Feast of Pentecost
May 1992

⟨❧⟩

Dearest Friends,

A few weeks ago, just as I was beginning my visit to the United States and Canada, news of one of the most important of all scientific discoveries ever made flashed briefly across the headlines. The theory that the universe began with a Big Bang about fifteen billion years ago received important confirmation from the discovery of radiation originating from a few cosmic moments after the Day of Creation. Everything we know in time and space came out of that primal explosion.

The scientists were ecstatic about their discovery. They spoke of having discovered the beginning of time, of having reached the edge of the universe; and finally, holding up a coloured picture of the cloud of radiation that gave rise to all this excitement, one of them said 'this is a picture of God'.

For many years now physicists have been searching for a unified field theory which will express the basic laws that unify the forces of nature. This latest discovery brings that goal closer. At the same time, it reminds us of the different levels of consciousness on which scientific discovery and spiritual vision take place.

The 'edge of the universe' has perhaps been photographed and we may be able to measure the beginning of time – and this is exciting and important – but the spiritual exploration of reality, which unites the inner and outer manifestations of God, meets a horizon rather than an edge. The horizon is real and perceptible but it is always receding. It is the point of departure as well as the destination. The journey of meditation is the journey home, the process of awakening to where we are, always have been and where we timelessly belong. The pilgrimage of meditation reveals, through experience rather than theory, that each of us is an intrinsic part of the unified field of God.

The meeting of science and religion in our time is healing one of the great divisions of the modern mind. Today indeed it is often the dedicated physicist who shows more real reverence, humility and joyful wonder in his or her contemplation of reality, than the over-stressed and sceptical administrator of organised religion. On the other hand, the great scriptural traditions remind the scientist that the universe cannot be studied realistically without accounting for the mystery of human consciousness. They show that the whole universe is embodied in the human being and that body, mind and spirit are not separate forms of energy. St Gregory Palamas wrote that the human being is 'the concentration of all that is, the recapitulation of all things created by God'.

The ordinary meditator can be helped by these deep changes in our culture and religious mentality. A feeling of foolishness, a sense of failure or discouragement, for example, often undermines the commitment to daily meditation. This can be challenged by the new sense of wonder awakening among us today, which is such a source of hope for our planet as well as of healing for our psyche. We can be reminded that what is foolish is not to give time and space to see beyond time and space. It is foolishness to have almost lost the gift of paying pure attention without counting the cost or calculating a return. Nothing is more foolish than to let the ego's petty obsession with success and failure deter us from finding our true self in union with God. 'The fool has said in his heart, there is no God above,' as the Hebrew poet sang thousands of years ago.

The deepest and unfathomable wonder of creation is not in what can be measured but in what can be listened to at both the innermost and the outermost reaches: the silence of God.

The recent election here in Britain and the one being fought in America at present, bring home to us how dangerously unsilent we have become. Without silence, all our communication systems, even our daily language, begin to deteriorate and can so easily become the tool for tyranny and deception. A medieval rabbi once wrote about the 'law of white spaces' in his commentary on the meaning of the Bible. The words of the text reveal an important meaning of God, he said. But it is the white spaces between the words that reveal the deepest meaning.

Without the ability to express ourselves we become the victims and prisoners of our own fears. We become obsessed with our limitations and forget our potential. But then language brings us to a higher level of awareness which enables us to see beyond words – into a silence that is the goal of, not a regressive escape from, human development. Silence gives us the courage to face a crisis in the most effective way of all, by abandoning thought, after we have done the necessary thinking, and by becoming still. Silence is the antidote for the chronic distractedness of our culture which erodes sensitivity and compassion and creates all the dangers of uncontrolled egoism.

One of the great crises of our time is the tragedy of the loss of a religious language and of a shared body of religious symbols. For Christianity the language of the scriptures has been largely invalidated as a means of communicating the faith to others. Fundamentalists, literalists and legalists in all denominations have even made it difficult to speak of 'Jesus Christ' outside of a church building without embarrassing the hearers. If silence restores us to the source of meaning, meditation returns us to the presence of Jesus.

There are stages of faith in Jesus. These stages are all 'true' and necessary, forming a single journey. We move in the New Testament, for example, from the more historical and chronological account of the life of Jesus of the synoptic Gospels; to the sense of his deeper meaning and identity in St John; to the Letters, especially of St Paul, and the breakthrough into the vision of the cosmic Christ.

Perhaps we should begin the journey of faith today by thinking of Jesus the meditator, not only Jesus the mediator. The early Gospels show Jesus pursuing his own unique human journey into self-knowledge, as a person who progressively 'increased in wisdom and in favour with God and with people' (Luke 2:52). This aspect of Jesus exerts a perennial fascination on us, even in a post-Christian society, as works like *Jesus Christ Superstar* or *The Last Temptation of Christ* have shown. The churches often show distaste and disapproval for such interest because it seems too irreverently to concentrate on the human side of Jesus. But without this bond to his humanity, faith cannot hope to develop into love, and then on to the next two stages which permit us to meet Jesus as the Saviour and as the cosmic Christ. Jesus prayed. He was part of a tradition in which he studied, was shaped, and prayed in many ways. His identity formed. Like every human life, his was impelled by a search for wholeness and unity, and it led him to self-knowledge.

Cardinal Newman wrote that 'a great proportion of what is generally received as Christian truth is, in its rudiments or in its separate parts, to be found in non-Christian philosophies and religions'. Our awareness of this has increased as our familiarity with other religions has deepened. It has often been a cause of worry and fear to Christians who see the uniqueness of their faith being eroded. In fact, it serves to deepen our faith, by restoring us to its basic essential: the self-knowledge of Jesus.

The natural human journey of Jesus led him to the unique awareness of his origin and meaning. 'I know where I come from and where I am going' (John 8:14). Each of us is called to this same self-discovery. We come to it by following him in his self-transcendence of his ego. 'Like us in all things but sin', the Mass tells us. Scripture shows us his struggle with himself, his temptations, his fears and grief. Without these experiences, over the whole spectrum of human feeling, he could not be like us. But unlike us he did not fall for the illusions of substitute wholeness – power, success or security – into which we so

frequently collapse because we identify so readily with our ego
and our fears and cravings.

Jesus' self-knowledge was so complete that it became inseparable from the knowledge of God ('Abba, Father'), of God
as the only true wholeness. Jesus rejected the imaginary worlds
of permanence which the ego constructs between itself and the
fear of death. He knew that the separate self must die, like
the grain of wheat, if the harvest of human selfhood is to grow.
The self-knowledge of Jesus is authenticated by his utter other-
centredness. He can be trusted with our lives because he can
say, 'The teaching that I give is not my own: it is the teaching
of him who sent me' (John 7:16). Because he does not aim at
his own honour he can be worshipped. This self-transcendent
dynamic of Jesus' self-knowledge is the deepest basis of Christian faith.

If it is true, as the theologians have said, that the Father sees
and loves in us what he sees and loves in the Son, it is no less
true that Jesus sees and loves in us what he sees and loves in
the Father, the Source. The self-knowledge of Jesus has centred
him in us as well as in God. Compassion is the sign of this. An
old Taoist saying says that 'heaven arms with compassion those
whom it would not see destroyed'. But, in Christianity, compassion is not only the true virtue and the fruit of meditation; it
is also revelatory of the very nature of God. Jesus' concern for
the underprivileged, the disadvantaged, all of history's failures,
has led to a unique Christian perspective of history. Meaning
and value are not restricted to the powerful, successful and
comfortable. Each human being is of supreme value.

This most revolutionary of all doctrines springs from the compassion of the human heart of Christ filled with his love of the
Father and his knowledge of himself. It is why meditation is still
the most revolutionary thing we can do, without doing violence
to ourselves or to others. Whichever way we go we will run
into this boundless compassion. We will find it whether we
seek God by asceticism, by restriction and separation or by
affirmation, by experimentation and expansion. There are dif-

ferent ways because there are different types of people. We all need to have the right kind of food, the bread of life, for the journey. There is no one else to meet and nowhere to meet him except in ourselves.

The goal of the Christian life is to know Jesus and through him to know God. We should not waste too much time defending particular definitions of him. What we usually defend in such cases are our own attachment to those definitions. Christianity is not a religion about the worship of Jesus. Jesus declared publicly: 'Whoever believes in me believes not in me, but in the one who sent me, and whoever sees me, sees the one who sent me. I have come into the world as light . . .' (John 12:44–6 NJB). Christianity is the celebration of this revelation of God, a religion of spirit and truth inspired by Jesus whose light shows us the 'kind of worshipper the Father seeks' (John 4:23 NJB).

This deep humility of Jesus the meditator prepares us to meet him 'as friends'. All the time we must be growing in self-knowledge so that we can be led by the Spirit to the next level of knowing Jesus – as Saviour. This word has almost been lost to modern vocabulary, despite the fact that politically we are always seeking a saviour, and that the world is widely networked by salvific movements such as the ecological, peace, justice and holistic movements. If we are to recover a sense of the specific Christian meaning of the word, our understanding of Jesus the meditator can be our preparation for it.

A saviour is one, like us, who seeks wholeness but who, unlike us, is not seduced by substitutes for God. He or she has encountered the basic human needs and accepted them as stages on the human ascent to wholeness. Above all, the saviour is one who is not afraid to die, or at least who is not mastered by their fear of death. They do not create 'immortality projects' to reinforce their denial of death, but live with the wisdom of mortality.

Sacrifice reveals its true meaning in the saviour. It is seen to be more than the substitute sacrifices we usually make to avoid the essential sacrifice of our ego. The saviour has discovered the interior meaning of sacrifice and shows it in his or her other-centred attention. Attention is the sacrifice offered on the altar of the heart, in which victim and priest are one. This is the 'life-giving law of the Spirit' that set St Paul 'free from the law of sin and death' (Romans 8:1–2).

The example of the saviour is the only true moral teaching. Without it we drift into making the false sacrifices of repression and denial. We are then never far from sacrificing others as our scapegoats. The saviour reveals that sacrificial love is the moral core of the universe. We are redeemed by love not by suffering. The cross of Jesus is the complete human symbol of this truth. There have been other great manifestations of God and they must all be reverenced. Each has something unique to teach us. But in Jesus we meet the Incarnation which Simone Weil described as the fulcrum by which the infinite God moves this finite world.

In some ways Jesus can be compared to what the Buddhists call a Bodhisattva. This is a perfected human being who does not totally transcend human life, so that he or she can continue to work for the perfection and liberation of others. In this spirit of compassion, Origen in the second century said that Christ will remain on the cross as long as a single creature remains in hell. His generous sense of the love of God even led him to believe that the devil would eventually be saved.

We are saved from the devil of our repressions and denials: from everything that impedes our complete sharing in the wholeness of God for which we were created. We are saved from the hell of isolation and from the inability to love. Jesus descended into this hell, touching the deepest levels of human misery with the knowledge of God from which his human consciousness could not be separated. We are saved by love. We are saved for love.

To have our faith grow into a knowledge of Jesus as saviour we need only open ourselves humanly to love. The unloving can know nothing of salvation, except perhaps their need for it. The question of how Jesus saves the world can only be approached once the primacy of love has been authentically accepted. This almost certainly means we have to have begun the transcendence of our own egoism before salvation can mean anything.

In the meantime we can use metaphors, like that of the ripple effect. Applying your foot to the brake on a crowded highway, they say, sends an effect back twenty-six miles in the chain of cars. At the deeper levels of human existence, where different laws – not just those of sin and death – apply, the love of God in Jesus ripples forwards and backwards in time and even beyond time.

In the same way that the salvific love of Jesus works through human nature, so does the effect of our own meditation. Any way of liberation must be liberating for others as well as for the one practising it. I cannot save myself at your expense. Meditation not only effects the supreme revolution of conversion of heart. It is also the most unselfish work we can perform and, in ways that may or may not be visible, it is manifested in the lives of others.

The disciples of Jesus share in his redemptive work for humanity, 'bearing fruit that will last' as he wished and predicted. Here we begin to glimpse how widely the dimensions of faith in Jesus can expand. Within a hundred years of their experiencing the Resurrection, his disciples were awakening to the fullest cosmic significance of their master. 'In Christ the complete being of the Godhead dwells embodied' (Colossians 2:9).

It soon became easy to confuse the cosmic Christ, whose form the disciples glimpsed in the light of the Resurrection, with worldly triumph. The triumphalism of princely ecclesiastical hierarchies, and of the inquisitions that imposed their power, travestied the Christ of the Letters to the Colossians and Ephesians. Here Jesus was seen, not only at the 'right hand of the Father', but equally within the heart of each of the Father's children.

The new challenge for Christianity is to recover a sense of

the cosmic Christ by finding the Christ within. This reuniting of Christian faith to its wholeness in Christ will assist the new synthesis of art, science and religion which is the new challenge faced by the world as a whole today.

We need to move beyond the images of Jesus to the deep inner reality of his presence. 'We however possess the mind of Christ', self-manifesting in the fruits of the spirit, the existential fruits of meditation. We pass through the stages of faith along which meditation guides us, knowing him, firstly, as one like ourselves, then as our saviour and, finally, as the Word through whom all that is came to be. This journey of faith is similar to the experience of turning a corner in a gallery, and finding oneself face to face with an original painting which, up to then, we have only known through reproductions. It is a moment of wonder, of recognition and new discovery. A timeless moment of presence.

With much love

Laurence

Laurence Freeman OSB

Letter Three

September 1992

Dearest Friends,

Part of each morning during the meditation retreat that we held at the Benedictine Abbey of Monte Oliveto Maggiore in Italy was devoted to *lectio* – a contemplative reading of scripture. One morning the *lectio* period took the form of a visual 'reading' of the frescoes of the life of St Benedict which were painted on the inner walls of the monastery cloister by the great Renaissance artists Signorelli and Sodoma. Robert Kiely led this visual *lectio*. I joined the session for some time before having to leave to prepare my talk for the day's conference. From my room where I was writing I could look down on the arches of the cloister and the garden it protected which was bathed in the fresh morning sunlight. I heard the quiet progress of the group over the worn stone floor as they moved from fresco to fresco through the life of St Benedict, and reflected on their own lives, just as generations of monks and pilgrims had done before them.

The beauty of it all was palpable, the kind that is difficult to describe without sentimentality! It was a moment of exceptional peace with a sense not so much of the transcendent glory of God as of the immanent order and tranquillity of the Spirit which Christ has breathed into our ordinary human lives. An order so easily lost and forgotten, superficially disordered or disrupted but never, at depth, absent. And in its permanence and faithful recurrences, redemptive of the ordinary.

From below I heard the murmur of teaching and discussion, a 'holy conversation' from which a flash of laughter would occasionally rise. Bob was pointing out how difficult it was in some of the frescoes to identify St Benedict himself, wearing the same white habit as his monks and merged with them in whatever incident was taking place to shape them and reveal the truth lying hidden in the ordinary, shot through with the extraordinary.

One memorable detail of a fresco, showing the monks at table with Benedict, has a monk slyly moving his hand across the table to steal the bread of the monk beside him. As if nothing were wrong, he is looking away from the deed, his little betrayal, but his neighbour is watching him with disappointment and amusement, his hand raised, just slightly, to slap the other's hand in the moment of theft. In its smallness and ordinariness the fresco gives a great teaching of compassion as it portrays a very human community of love that accepts each member in a divine way just as they are.

The knowledge that we are accepted like this is redemptive. It transforms us. Knowing that our psychological flaws and per-sonality defects do not automatically earn us the punishment which we expect and fear and which we so often inflict upon ourselves simply stops us in our tracks. It brings us to that unexpected resting place which is the turning-point of conver-sion. The gift of forgiveness, though it contains everything we are seeking, is only a beginning. We doubt it, test it, betray the truth again and again to see whether we will be punished this time. As sinners we are always hurt children. As saints we are the same children at last wholly reassured by love.

Love does everything which we separate in our minds into different functions of our relationship with God: it creates; it nurtures, evolves and guides; it redeems; it roots and trans-cends; it corrects and it heals. In the Christian revelation of the meaning of love meditation is the power of prayer that holds our attention at the still point of conversion, where we are shocked into reality by acceptance. By being rooted in this place of transformation which is not geographical but spiritual, our own inmost centre, we are changed from being an approximation, an imitation of ourselves, into the exact original of who we are.

'I implore you by God's mercy to offer your very selves to him: a living sacrifice, dedicated and fit for his acceptance, the worship offered by mind and heart. Adapt yourselves no longer to the pattern of this present world, but let your minds be remade and your whole nature thus transformed' (Romans 12:1–2).

The life of the spirit in human nature is a continual repatterning. The step of faith we spend our lives perfecting is simply the one step by which we let our minds be remade and our whole being transfigured. For 'this present world' let us read 'ego': the part that thinks it is the whole. It has come involuntarily to block and unconsciously to distort the mystery of life because of the patterns it has formed through pain and rejection; the perception of a world without love.

At the memorable Seminar Jean Vanier led in London in June, just before the Monte Oliveto retreat, he spoke with deep wisdom of the causes of these patterns of pain. He opened a deeper vision for us of the sacredness of human wounds, describing them as the points of vulnerability where the love of Jesus touches the human person and by healing transforms us into children of God. Jean's own life and his L'Arche family of communities for the mentally handicapped teach us this primary gospel truth of poverty. And by teaching this they liberate us, like prayer itself, from false images of God.

In so many painful ways today western people have become imprisoned in the patterns of their personalities, sources of their own suffering and complicated systems of self-rejection. We have, perhaps more than ever before, identified ourselves with our ego and adopted its values as the forces that determine our works, our relationships, and so our societies.

When the early Christians spoke of separating themselves from the world, it was not God's creation they were escaping from but the prison of a consciousness that had slipped into the chasm of the ego. Today we may talk more readily of freeing

the parameters of our personality. We are unhappy with ourselves; and unless we can find a spiritual path to the other
shore, a spiritual ladder up out of the abyss, we fall into false
paths that only tighten the knots of the heart the more we try
to untie them.

What we take to be our 'selves' are more often the conditioned patterning of our personalities, shaped by genes, parental personalities and history. There is no self we can know of
that does not become expressed through a personality. Wisdom
consists in seeing the distinction between the personality and
the Self. It is each day's challenge and the great ordeal of our
life to see with this clarity.

Personality is patterned both genetically and psychologically.
It is ours, uniquely and irreplaceably. It can be transformed,
integrated, but never exchanged. If we are dissatisfied with it
or if it has become a source of suffering for us, it is the height
of folly to try to destroy it or to superimpose a better one onto it.
We can only change by accepting ourselves. Sin that is punished
hides and, if defeated, takes on new shapes, but sin forgiven
is transmuted into freedom. This is the task both of human
relationships and of prayer.

The patterns of response and perception that form the personality, our ego-identity, in our formative years overlap and interweave. Some that arise from our deeper experiences of
suffering become deeply engrained patterns of guilt, fear, rejection. Patterns can change shape like clouds without ceasing to
be engrained, as when a pattern of rejection turns into a pattern
of addiction, or one of fear into another of cruelty. The Bible
well knew that the human soul perplexes any attempt to understand or predict it.

Adapt yourselves no longer to the patterns of this present
world, St Paul told the early Christians in the house churches
of Rome. The way to do so is essentially the same for us as for
them: prayer and an ordered life, as St Benedict taught his lay
communities of monks and oblates. The meditation group is
simply another form of the community of faith – prayer and

praxis – in which the mind can be remade and our nature transformed. To work on the patterns of the personality that block or paralyse us we must sink deeper than the personality, the ego, into our true personhood, the self or spirit. In this centre of our being we are unconditioned; no pattern is superimposed on us. Here we are free, with the 'glorious liberty of the children of God'. Here the fruits of the Spirit reside in us in pure potency: love, joy, peace, patience and all those qualities of human wholeness which St Paul says are subject to no law whatsoever. In our spirit we are simply our selves: being in communion. There is no patterning because there is no before or after, no action and therefore no reaction. Being present to itself, as the mystics said; yet not a reality for the few but as close to us all as the present moment; not a reward for virtue or work well done but the pure gift of unconditional love that includes even what tries to deny it.

Even if meditation were no more than a brief daily dip into the kingdom within us it would merit our complete attention. But it is more than a temporary escape from the prison of our patterns of fear and desire. Complex as these patterns are, making us fear the death and the true love that are necessary for our growth and survival, meditation simplifies them all. Day by day, meditation by meditation, this process of simplification proceeds. We become gradually more fearless until in the joy of being released from the images and memories of desire we taste total freedom from fear. And then – and even before then – we become of use to others, able to love without fear or desire and having our personalities released to serve the Self which is the Christ within.

It all is and yet it is to come. We live each day within the process of transformation, the remaking of the Spirit. The gap between the Self and the ego-centred personality may not be real. Everything is contained in the spirit including the mortal life of the personality. But we feel the gap nonetheless as a painful, sometimes accusatory, absence of integrity. Flashes of

joy may be felt but also there are flashes of anger and destructiveness, the great refusal of the ego to bow before the Self.

For many people their early religious conditioning set up patterns of self-rejection in response to these dark flashes of sin.
They were felt to be signs of the inherent degeneracy of human
nature in the fallen state. People were taught to focus on them
as the sign of what they were truly like. This self-accusation was
explained as the meaning of the great contemplative wisdom of
'know thyself'. To this day many people begin the sacrament
of reconciliation with the words 'I accuse myself'.

No doubt we are meant to change the patterns of sin – fear,
fantasy, addiction and selfishness. But we are no less enjoined
by the gospel to break the patterns of religious response that
trap us in cycles of self-rejection and guilt. The destructive patterns of the personality are broken not by punishment or
repression but by unflinching forgiveness and unwavering
acceptance. These tools of love given by the God who loves
good and bad alike are the strongest weapon in the human
arsenal. Those who hold power and authority over the moral
and spiritual lives of others, the keys of the kingdom, forget this
core truth of the gospel at their peril and at the peril of the
church. It is only too easy to condemn, punish, silence or
excommunicate those we genuinely believe to be at fault. By
doing so we may be doing well by an institution, but we are
stealing the bread of love from our neighbour's hand and from
the church which is the table where this bread is meant to be
shared.

Patterns of selfishness or destructiveness do not show the
rottenness of human nature. Even the horrors we see and read
of in civilised Europe, the murders in Belfast and the camps in
Bosnia, are not proofs of evil nature. Perhaps life would be
easier if they were, if forgiveness were really an impolitic weakness and if evil could really never be redeemed. But in these
horrors, as in our own daily betrayals of truth or love, we see
only flashes out of the dark, fearsome pits of the soul which are
unenlightened, unloved, unconscious of having been redeemed.

We see in them, as well as in our reaction to them, patterns that cry out to be 'remade'. Precisely because they are patterns and because they can recur long after we think we have been freed from them, they can weaken our hope and lead us to despair. 'Can I ever change?' 'Will the world never learn?'

I recently saw a wonderful production of Sophocles' Theban plays, telling the tragic story of Oedipus and his family. The mystery of human life with all its conflicting elements of good and evil, joy and suffering, treachery and nobility was as present to the Greek mind 2,500 years ago as it is to us today. But in the poetry of the Greeks we witness the wonder of the mind awakening for the first time to itself, to the power of thought and language, to the Logos and the awareness that action carries moral meaning. The freshness of this awakening is exhilarating. But it makes us aware today that we have lived with these discoveries, and the patterns of thought they set up in us, for many generations: above all the pattern of thinking that thought is the greatest human power. Looking back on the road humanity has travelled for so long helps us to see that we too are on the brink of a self-discovery every bit as astonishing as that of the Greeks.

The Greeks witnessed the dawn of reason. With its bright light today we can see the dawning of a spiritual life not only in individuals, where it has always been, but in the human family as a whole. This is the 'new age', not of the post-religious societies of the western world, but of the kingdom described and revealed by Jesus and the world's prophets before him. No one has described more humanly than Jesus that the power of this kingdom is not thought, or physical force, or psychic wonders, but love.

The patterns of the minds change within us when as individuals we open ourselves to this deepest of all powers. To meet it we have to let go of all our understanding and definition of love. We have, even more painfully for most of us, to let go of the desire for love that our woundedness makes so dominant within our personalities. But these patterns also change in the human family as a whole while the Spirit guides creation along its stages of evolution. Collectively, too, we have to meet the supreme reality of love through the pain of letting go of the temples we have built: temples of stone as well as the temples of the mind with their beautiful cathedrals of thought and dogma (compare John 4:21–6).

To say we are moving beyond the world of thought does not mean we are regressing into pre-rational consciousness. That is still with us, as Belfast and Bosnia show. Beyond thought there is spirit. Nor do the changing patterns of religious life and practice in our society mean that we are becoming totally Godless. There has always been much practising atheism in religious institutions. But beyond religion, too, there is the Spirit.

To transcend is the first step in growth. The essential second step is then to integrate what has been transcended. It can be painful or tedious but it must be done before we can move on to the new stage. To say we are moving beyond thought does not mean we will stop thinking. Because the influence of religious institutions is waning does not mean that religious traditions or all their structures will disappear. They will, however, be repatterned, just as the human being is changed in the course of a lifetime. Tragedy strikes, as the Greeks were the first to see, when human beings cling to their own egocentric patterns and resist the greater pattern of the higher powers.

What rises falls, and even in destruction God works the mystery of rebirth. But wisdom is given us to co-operate rather than to fight this progressive cycle of change; and to grow with the minimum of suffering and the least waste of human effort. It was this spirit of wisdom that descended on Pope John XXIII and that Christians, who have all been touched by this event regardless of their own tradition, need still to be faithful to. The liberation of Christianity into its new era does not just concern Christians. If it did it would not be so important. It certainly does not just concern the administrators or the teachers of Christian religion. If it did it would hardly be important at all. It concerns the whole human family in its walk towards God. Not only because of the association of Christianity with the world's dominant western culture, but because of a mystery of universality – not exclusivity – that is at the very heart of Christian faith.

The repatterning of our minds which St Paul urges on the ordinary people of the early churches is the result of transcendence and integration. Meditation is such a powerful practice in the human process and a permanent gift in the human family of such mystery because it takes us directly in to the heart of this transformation. As modern people at the limit of rational development – not just intellectuals but as people of our cerebral culture – we long to understand how this happens. We even try to measure it and invent scientific methods to rationalise it. That does no harm to meditation which still patiently waits for us to take the necessary step of faith beyond thought. The mantra is this little step, taken once so that it can be taken again and again. It is in the littleness, the powerlessness of the mantra that its great potency is found. By its total commitment to letting go it releases the power of faith in us that moves the mountain of the ego.

Saying the mantra and letting go of all thoughts and imagination, rich and wonderful as they are, is like walking on water. It seems impossible, as it did to Peter on the Lake of Galilee, but it is still what we are strangely called to do. When our attention falters, when we 'doubt', we sink into thought and only when we are lifted up out of it, into a fuller consciousness, can we start again. Distractions, and returning to the mantra, teach us as nothing more simple can, that there is something greater than thought, a state more fully alive than thinking about life.

Another of the frescoes at Monte Oliveto tells the story of Maurus and Placid, two disciples of St Benedict. Maurus is sent to rescue Placid from drowning. Obeying without hesitation or self-consciousness, Maurus runs across the water to fulfil his task and bring his friend back to shore. At the end of the story Placid tells how he 'saw' Benedict in Maurus at the moment of his rescue. The fresco of course is able to show all this simultaneously, the sending of Maurus, the walking on water, the perception of Placid of the union of consciousness between master and disciple. All the stages are represented as a unity. Maurus was amazed at what he had done. It could not have been his own miracle, he said, because he did not even know he was performing it!

The mantra leads to an obedience of simple union in which the miracle of life is worked deep within us beyond the power of thought to observe it. We are letting go of the power of thought in favour of the power of love. 'God cannot be known by thought but only by love.' In love's power our minds are freed from the patterns of the past and our whole being is filled with the wholeness of God.

With much love

Laurence

Laurence Freeman OSB

Letter Four

March 1993

Dearest Friends

It is difficult to be writing anything in England right now without relating it to a tragedy which is still stunning the country. The killing of a two-year-old after his abduction by two ten-year-old children has horrified everyone. It has touched the nerve of the nation even more deeply than the worst atrocities reported here from Bosnia or Somalia in recent months, precisely because it has happened in the most unthinkable place – at home. The sense of collective shame and guilt goes deep and wide; and even when the newspapers have moved on to another story, one feels that the imprint of this event on the social psyche will remain potent.

Ordinary people, including parents of ten-year-olds, are asking what very unsettling and disturbing truths we are being taught about our society. Its culture of violence and alienation, it seems, is bearing the fruits of evil in the minds and behaviour of the very young, not only the naturally rebellious adolescent. One of the most uneasy aspects of the moment is that there is no adequate forum or authority on which to base the self-scrutiny it demands. Even the intelligent newspapers reflecting on the story carry advertisements in the same issue for the film *Terminator 2*. Politicians can hardly forbear making political points when they discuss its implications. One wonders where the shepherds of religion are as the spiritual famine of the people is exposed. Mostly, I'm afraid, discussing what to do with the

male priests who want to leave their church because of the ordination of women.

A few weeks ago in the far north of Britain an oil tanker ran
aground and spilled its load. The pictures of oil-covered seals
and seabirds pathetically showed the unresolved conflict in our
world between technology and the environment. But human
tragedies, especially those showing engrained social patterns
affecting the young, flash a warning to us of an even more
insidious though invisible pollution of the human mind.

One word that the politicians and media do not use in discussing all this is 'spiritual'. Yet the wisdom of the ages is that
the spiritual traditions of all the religions contain the only real
antidote for the pollution of consciousness or 'sin'. In spiritual
practice, in 'prayer', human consciousness is purified and clarified so that in self-knowledge it can become aware of its true
nature, and mirror the qualities of its divine source.

As we meditate, alone or in weekly groups or in communities,
we can hardly not grow more aware of the deep relation
between meditation and the world in which we live. Out of
this awareness there grows an experience of relatedness – the
ground of being in which we are all rooted – which expresses
itself in a heightened sense of responsibility. Our natural con-
science then guides us to act responsibly in the appropriate
area of our life and in this we celebrate the marriage of contemplation and action. The power that drives this process is love.
Compassion is love uniting those who suffer. It is redemptive
because, against every expectation, it strikes a light in the dark-
est depth and releases the joy of being at the heart of the worst
of tragedies. But this is the kind of redemption that it is useless
to talk about before it has been felt.

The collective reaction to a national tragedy can reveal the
universal capacity for compassion in human nature. While this
capacity is fulfilled we are able to see life in perspective. True
values displace false ones. The impatience and intolerance that
arise from fear between peoples die down and we treat each
other in those moments of grace with sympathy and respect.

The kingdom, Christians could say, is at hand; its interiority has become manifest in human relationships. But we know sadly that such moments of peace do not last long. Destructive and self-interested criticism and backbiting, gossip and cunning, are quick to resume their sway over personal and social relations. Within religious groups, no less than in any other.

One meaning of suffering and evil is surely that it does draw us, however briefly, into the shared awareness of the reality of communion. We see that the kingdom (or its eastern parallels, *nirvana* and *samadhi*) is not a product to be produced and consumed but the timeless and boundless ground of being. Provided we have not become desensitised to suffering, which our screen-culture threatens, we glimpse in tragedy not only how distant but how close God is to us.

There is in us clearly a terrible capacity for collective cruelty, if even 'ethnic cleansing' can be bureaucratically organised in a country that had until recently been a holiday tour-operators' paradise. Yet the self-contradiction of human nature shows that there is no less a collective facility for shame and guilt. Even though in blaming and condemning others for their crimes we risk the more subtle sin of the Pharisees, we cannot in our inmost self help recognising that every crime implicates us all.

The schoolmaster who punishes the whole class represents not God (who forgives the whole class) but the law of karma, what St Paul called the 'law of sin and death', the deep-structure truth of original sin. Christian morality has long been confused by identifying the schoolmaster with God. The law of karma in Indian philosophy is also one of the great insights of the Semitic religions, expressed in the biblical idea of sin. But the punishment of sin is a process of created nature, not an attribute of the divine nature. God, in other words, does not punish. Our own deeds punish us, and the consequences of our actions, as we see in the tragic deformation of the young, cannot be limited to the individual.

God does not punish nor, strictly speaking, does God forgive. God is. All divine action is present in the single act of Being. It is, by its nature, purely loving. And it is unflinchingly constant in its relationship (which is not outside itself) with us in all our moody and vagrant behaviour. Forgiveness is the human discovery of the constancy of the divine being of love. It is the encounter of human guilt with divine innocence. Jesus is the story of this.

If there is a collective capacity both for evil and shame, there must (one hopes) be a collective capacity for good. Our modern sense of this capacity has been undermined and weakened. This is partly due to the way the media, in their still childish attempt to mirror the oneness of the human family, treats good news. They condescend to goodness, treating examples of natural kindness and generosity as cloying sweeteners at the end of news broadcasts of unrelieved gloom and doom. Artists and journalists alike have usually found the good to be boring. The bad excites. And we have not yet learned to deal morally with the economic discovery that excitement sells.

Religion in its institutionalised sense is usually associated with looking good and being on one's best behaviour. This is one reason why religion is generally felt by the young to be boring and makes many feel that it is inherently hypocritical. The role models of the young are often very flawed and damaged human beings, like the rock stars, who are far from exemplary but who neither pretend nor aspire to be better than others. Their virtue is honesty and sincerity rather than good behaviour. With religious people it is often the exact reverse.

The insight that the surface and depth of our personalities are closely related and affect each other is vital for human growth. But it can be dangerous. It can lead us to think that if we look good we can be good. Or that if we do good then we must be good. Religion becomes the principal barrier between us and God as soon as it fails to be rigorously centred in the inner nature, the being of humanity, and instead becomes primarily concerned with the surface, with appearances and with public behaviour. The sign that religion has become wrongly centred is that it preaches too much. To preach means to be always telling people what to do and what not to do. The style of preaching matters little, whether aggressive or passive. Human beings instinctively dislike being preached at. So, unless the preacher has some hold over us, we will eventually abandon him in his pulpit to preach to other preachers, or relish his reduction to the level of the rest of humanity.

The role of religion is to teach, not preach. The role of the minister is to initiate rather than legislate. If this is even partly true, all the churches (to speak only of Christianity) must, like Peter, face the fact of their betrayal. Instead of feeling betrayed by their congregations or complaining of the disloyalty of their clergy, religion today needs to assess how guilty it is of betraying the real spiritual needs of society. The clarity of that awakening will be the empowerment of religion to teach, heal and serve.

A great modern philosopher, Ludwig Wittgenstein, once wrote in the foreword to a book that half of what he wanted to say was in the words of the book. The other half was said in silence. Modern Christianity needs to learn again the art of the sermon of silence.

True silence exposes the mock silences that try to conceal the evasion or distortion of the truth. We do this in our personal communication with each other no less than in our social inter- course. The chattering media are full of this false silence, which is why they dare not leave a moment or space unfilled for fear that the emptiness might release the silence of truth. We do it daily in our homes and communities and offices whenever we disobey St Benedict who warned us not to 'give a false peace'. The Book of Leviticus shows the true biblical sense of sin when it tells us that we take sin upon ourselves when we fail to confront others with their offences against us and when we harbour grudges in our hearts. Sin, in other words, most danger- ously erupts and finds its most favourable conditions in the dynamics of psychological repression. The sins of the prosti- tutes and tax-collectors, as Jesus taught us, are minute com- pared with those of the righteous. In the face of atrocities we automatically tend to shout our outrage. Crowds shout and cannot listen. The medley of personas and conversations in the unsilent mind is itself a crowd that cannot listen. If, however, we can see how unnatural evil in all its dark fruits really is, and if we can understand how silent nature is, we can learn the redemptive and purifying power of silence. Whatever is simply itself is silent. It does not matter whether it is talking or quacking or blowing in the wind. Silence is not influenced by noise if the noise does not pretend anything or try to take over anything else's identity or right to be. When the habit of meditation is integrated into daily life it becomes easier to meditate in noisy places, and even to regard the internal noise of mental distractions with the same kind of detachment as external noise.

Silence purifies. It restores us to our true nature and reverses the counter-currents of the unnatural. Reappropriating our true nature in meditation means that by meditating we learn to meet the basic needs of our nature. By 'meeting our needs', I mean both senses of meeting – firstly, encountering them, then fulfilling them. We cannot fulfil them until we have fully faced and accepted them; until we can recognise our needs without feelings of guilt or self-rejection. These are human needs like wholeness, happiness and peace. They are not abstractions. And they are not desires. In silence they become known and accepted as real processes in our own nature. John Main said that meditation helps us to verify the truths of our faith. In the great discernment between needs and desires which silence brings us to, we are restored to a direct and harmonious relationship, a non-duality, with ourselves. The only victim of this is the phantom of our imagined self and its fears and illusions.

Meditation sharpens our sense of how many unnatural forces are at work today. War, racial and religious vendettas, the exploitation of the innocent, the fascination with the perverse and the addiction to violence leave none of us unaffected, but the young are the most vulnerable. A society that thinks it can deal with this deviation from natural needs merely by force of punishment or repression is headed for catastrophe.

The alienation from our own spiritual – boundless and compassionate – nature can only be corrected by learning again what our true nature is. Returning to nature does not mean just country walks, but it can be as arduous and as refreshing as physical exercise. Meditation restores a healthy appetite for life in place of the decadent fascination with death and corruption. We see it in the love of life of the holy ones, the saint's inability to be bored. The work of silence similarly reminds us that we must find our greatest pleasures in what is natural. Only in harmony with our own nature, physical, mental and spiritual, can we awaken to God who is the author of all nature. Such is the power of the law of self-knowledge.

God is in nature – what simply is – yet also free of it. Therefore, by finding our true nature, created in the image of God with our consciousness mirroring and partaking of the divine consciousness, we experience both peace and liberty. The peace arises from the certain knowledge that our very nature is rooted in God and is as real as God. It is the all-empowering peace of belonging to what we know will never reject or disown us, the self-confidence of love. Liberty springs from the joy of transcendence, of knowing that what we belong to belongs to us. Rootedness allows expansion, just as St Benedict's vow of stability permits continuous transformation.

What is natural is ordinary. The simple discipline of meditation, when it is followed without demands for experiences or expectation of rewards, opens a dimension of awareness which remains closed as long as we judge it only by visible results. We learn, through practice, to develop and sustain the right approach to meditation. There is no technique to master, no theory to understand. There is, therefore, neither success nor failure. This attitude to the mantra deepens the purifying power of the silence and itself becomes the attitude we bring to life as a whole. St Paul taught the importance of being a 'cheerful giver': 'there should be no reluctance, no sense of compulsion'. This is the state of balance in which, for example, the virtue (the spiritual strength) of patience is learned.

Learning a new computer recently brought me to the brink of rage as I managed to jam it completely so that no key responded. It was the type of experience of frustration that drives us to violence. Controlled, we can laugh at it. Over the edge we fall into the abyss. In this instance I was eventually humbled enough to read the manual, where I discovered the existence of a minute hole on the machine called, redemptively, 'reset'. By inserting a very fine pin into the aperture the theologically minded operator could experience forgiveness. Everything, in the twinkling of a microchip, was restored to innocence and a fresh start.

If the aperture we must find in ourselves is the heart, the sharp point which enters it and releases the energy of renewal is the word. Human life both individually and collectively can get jammed. Rather than rage, the teachers of wisdom have shown us compassion and patience in the face of our mistakes. And above all they have pointed to the spiritual path of the heart. In prayer, rather than intellect or activity by themselves, we find the essential humanising – or rehumanising – power.

In the face of our contemporary crises we need to ask why we meditate. We ask it not to undermine our commitment but to refine and deepen it. We are not in pursuit of interesting experiences. Meditation is not information technology. It is about knowledge that redeems, pure consciousness – knowing, not merely knowing about. Meditation does not increase our funds of information. In fact we turn away from our usual information-gathering and sorting as we turn to a knowledge which is not quantifiable and which unifies rather than analyses. The feeling of foolishness or of being unproductive is a positive sign that we are being led to the 'spiritual powers of wisdom and vision, by which there comes the knowledge of him' (Ephesians 1:17). This redemptive and recreative knowledge is the wisdom our age lacks. We can recognise it and discriminate between it and its counterfeits because it neither claims nor parades any possessive pronoun. No one claims it as their own. It is not 'his or her, my or your' knowledge.

It is the consciousness of the Holy Spirit and therefore it is the womb of all truly loving action. In the face of the most disheartening tragedy it is as close to us as we are to our true selves.

Let us continue to keep Fr Bede in his illness in our hearts, as well as his community at the ashram of Shantivanam. Fr Bede has lit the way for so many who have been seeking a way to live a spiritual and full life in the modern world. And he has taught us that however difficult the gift of life may be it must always be accepted and loved because it is naturally good.

With much love

Laurence

Laurence Freeman OSB

Letter Five

June 1993

Dearest Friends,

Father Bede Griffiths died peacefully at his ashram at Shanti-vanam at about 4.15 p.m. on 13 May. Br Martin, Fr Christadas, Sr Marie-Louise and others of his community who had so lovingly cared for him in his illness were beside him as he took this last step on his pilgrimage.

In March I visited him for a week at the spiritually based medical centre in Kerala where he was receiving a month of traditional Indian therapy. One of the daily treatments, called dhara, involved his being laid on a long wooden pallet for massage. During the massage a stream of milk mixed with healing herbs flowed over the upper part of his head from a bowl suspended a few inches above him and constantly replenished by an attendant.

To western eyes it seemed at first a strange and rather undignified treatment of a frail old man. But the profound calm of the way it was administered and the way Fr Bede himself accepted it as part of the total integration of his being which he felt was happening to him, helped me to see it later in the week as a kind of anointing. It seemed that his long and mysterious relationship with Christ in India was being consummated in this rite. Although it was like a rite of extreme unction it was also a kind of baptism. India was baptising him with itself, the India he had come to forty years before in order, as he said, 'to find the other half of my soul'.

Unlike previous missionaries who came only to baptise India,

Fr Bede was bathed by India. Yet the wonder is that the great expansion of mind and heart that India and the other eastern religions worked in him served at the end of his life to deepen and clarify his own centredness in Christ. Love of Jesus and wonder at the cosmic Christ, the personal and universal dimensions of Christianity, reached a rare peak and integration in him in these days. It reminded me again that faith is essentially a personal transmission. The institution exists primarily to prepare the ground and conditions for holiness.

Two days after Fr Bede passed wholly into God I met with His Holiness the Dalai Lama at a Tibetan monastery in Scotland. In 1980 he had come to visit Fr John at our first small home on Vendome Avenue in Montreal. He had meditated with us and stayed for lunch, after which he and Fr John met and talked. The strangeness of the circumstances of the present encounter seemed a commentary on the 'marriage of East and West' which the Spirit is guiding in such diversity and unity around the globe. The thriving Buddhist monastic community in Scotland, its planned college and the acquisition of Holy Island off the Arran coast as a retreat centre, all point to a new era and intensity of religious awareness and perhaps of spiritual experience. We are on the threshold of something of which Thomas Merton, John Main, Bede Griffiths, the Dalai Lama are each a prophet in a unique way. To discover its full significance is the greatest adventure of our time.

The Dalai Lama and I talked for nearly an hour and I would like to make this newsletter a way of sharing with our Community of Christian meditators as much as words can convey of his wisdom and insight, compassion and tolerance. I asked him about his approach to meditation (we will all be consoled to know that even he finds one-pointedness difficult!), his views on the meeting of religions and his feelings about the future of Tibet. What the written responses cannot capture is his humour and deep-voiced laughter or the sense he gives of a strong, finely tuned inner balance between seriousness and playfulness.

Perhaps what the words can convey is a sense of why so

many westerners today find in him their most authoritative and
approachable symbol of spiritual leadership. Part of the reason
for this, no doubt, as with Fr Bede's authority, is his lack of a
sense of dogmatic righteousness. He does not use right and
wrong as clubs of guilt but as pointers to enlightenment. Buddhism is more existential than theological, although you can
glimpse the intricate philosophy of Buddhism. But generally the
Buddhist approach is practical. 'Helpful' and 'useful' are words
the Dalai Lama likes to use. A spiritual path is composed of
'skillful means'. Fr Bede found Christ in the other half of his
Indian soul. It would be a dull Christian who would not feel
his or her faith sharpened and vitalised by the Buddhism of the
Dalai Lama, one of the great wisdom traditions of the human
family.

Conversation with the Dalai Lama

at Samye Ling Monastery, Eskdale Muir, Dumfriesshire,

15 May 1993

Q. What is the role that meditation plays in your own life?

A. Oh, very important. In fact I think it is the most important
thing. Meditation is essential in order to transform one's
spiritual life. In the Buddhist tradition one's future entirely
depends upon one's own actions. And action depends upon
motivation. At the level of motivation there is, by nature,
the human opposites of negative and positive emotion. By
positive I mean those emotions which lead to the actions
which ultimately bring happiness. The negative emotions, of
course, bring the opposite. Now, these negative emotions
are from birth. They come from an infinite beginning and are
part of our mind, and in order to remove them the positive
emotions must increase. For example, in order to reduce
hatred you must develop the opposite side such as compassion and kindness. So some kind of competition or conflict is always there. This or that side tries to minimise the
other side.

Due to a person's past experience the negative side is more forceful at the outset. Because the positive side is weaker at the beginning you have this competition or conflict. Now, through meditation the positive side is promoted. Meditation means making acquaintance with the positive side of thoughts or emotions. In that way you use it and increase its force. As this side increases in strength then automatically the negative side is reduced. That is the way of transformation for all. So in the Buddhist tradition meditation is very important. It is very crucial.

Q. How do you personally meditate every day?

A. In my daily prayer or meditation there is variety. There is this variety of course in all Buddhist practice and particularly among Mahayana Buddhist practitioners. But basically there are two kinds: analytical meditation and then single-pointedness of meditation. In my own experience in certain fields single-pointedness is very, very crucial. But in general analytical meditation can be very forceful – and also for me it is easier! The other is much more difficult.

Q. Why is it more difficult?

A. You see, for that practice you need at least a few months or at least a certain time of complete isolation, solitude. That is difficult. Firstly, analytical meditation addresses contentment: the realisation of the nature of worldly happiness and the nature of impermanence and of suffering. In the Buddhist view an increase of attachment results in samsara or cyclic existence. Meditation helps to reduce desire or attachment towards worldly things, including sex. Then, on the other hand, there is the analytical meditation on compassion. All other sentient beings are just like ourselves in wanting to overcome suffering and to have permanent happiness. Meditating on that nature increases our compassion. At the same time you can meditate on negativeness and for example analyse the nature of anger, particularly hatred. That is a major portion of my meditation. These are the common practices of meditation.

Q. In your role as the leader of the Tibetan people you must feel a strong anger against the Chinese for what they have done and are doing to your people. Yet part of the witness you make to the world is that you do not feel hatred. Would you describe this in Christian terms as loving your enemies? How does your meditation help you to feel anger without hatred? Is that what love of enemies means?

A. Oh yes. There is a particular form of practice known as giving and taking. One of the principal means of enhancing compassion and love is to apply this method. It involves visualising and imagining your giving your own positive qualities like happiness and your various virtuous thoughts and emotions toward others, and then taking upon yourself their sufferings and pains and particularly their negative emotions.

When I do this practice on a daily basis I pay special attention to our enemy the Chinese, particularly the Chinese who are actively involved in perpetrating these crimes against my people. You see we cannot categorise the Chinese as a whole as our enemy, only those individual Chinese who are responsible. So this is one form of practice that I do. I take upon myself the negativities, the emotions, the anger, the hatred that these Chinese have, upon myself and then I share; I send out my positive energies and thoughts and feelings towards these people. So it is a form of giving and taking. It is very useful. It is very effective.

Q. Do you feel that spiritual practices of this kind have a relevance to the world at large and the political field in which conflicts are being handled?

A. That I don't know. When I say it is important I mean important to me as a Buddhist practitioner. In my daily practice these practices are very important. They are useful.

Q. Is it realistic to think that it could be practised widely?

A. I don't know. You see, for this practice you need some other background practice. The Buddhist for example accepts the rebirth theory and the potential of all beings for Buddhahood. Things like these are specific to the background of Buddhist practice and they are all involved with each other. If you accept there is just one lifetime then things become much simpler! You asked me about my daily prayer so I explained it this way as a Buddhist!

Q. What would you say to a Christian thinking of becoming a Buddhist or a Buddhist thinking of becoming a Christian?

A. On that matter I usually tell people that it is very complicated. It is a big decision after all to change your religion and so you must be very cautious. Changing religion is not an easy thing. I have noticed some people who change religion and find big difficulties later on. So it is important to be very cautious. But if someone after careful thinking really feels that the new religion is more suitable then of course it is the individual's right to do so. That is usually my advice.

Q. How can a person be wholeheartedly committed to one path and yet also say 'I do not have a monopoly on the truth'?

A. From the Buddhist viewpoint there are many, many different aspects or levels of the Truth. There is a good example of this from the Buddhist standpoint and history. The Buddha was one teacher who taught different philosophy to different people. There are some very crucial points such as ultimate reality and ultimate truth on which Buddha taught differently with different explanations. These differences were not just minor but in some cases quite contradictory. From one viewpoint this belief, for example, is nihilism; from that viewpoint it is absolutism. So there is complete opposition, but both were taught by Buddha.

This tells me that Buddha respected the individual's mental disposition. For this particular person the Buddha found one explanation was more suitable for them. So for that person, for a certain period, it is for them the ultimate truth. So it is more useful and he therefore deliberately taught them that philosophy. What I learn from this is how easily I can view other or non-Buddhist traditions. Each one has a very good message or method to improve good human qualities. In different circumstances and under different aspects each religion has its truth.

Q. Is it possible then to be a Christian Buddhist or a Buddhist Christian?

A. Hmmm. At an initial stage this is possible. Someone who believes or sincerely respects both Jesus Christ and the Buddha can be considered as a half-Buddhist, half-Christian. But then, you see, with further spiritual development I don't think this can be so. The Buddhist practitioner has to accept that the important practice is emptiness. Some Christian brothers have showed me their keen interest in the Buddhist philosophy of emptiness. But I feel that if you accept emptiness then there is very little room except for Creator or Absolute. Emptiness means that everything is interdependent. From that philosophical viewpoint the acceptance of the permanent soul and an Absolute or Almighty is rather difficult.

Q. Is the experience, then, the same but the interpretation of it different?

A. It's quite difficult to generalise. One might even have to say that the experience might be different. If one is talking of quite a highly advanced realisational state, then at that point – and because there are such fundamental differences – it perhaps might not make sense to talk of experiences being one or the same.

Broadly speaking, an individual Christian may interpret the Creator in the context of relative nature. At the same time Creator can mean the basis of all phenomena. It may therefore depend upon the personal interpretation of individual practitioners. It is possible for some to have a concept of the Creator or creation within the understanding of a relative world without according any absolute status to an external being. The Creator then is not understood in the sense of a personal God as you find in the biblical tradition but rather in terms of the basis or foundation from which the entire mass of phenomena or evolution starts. For instance something can from a certain perspective be said to be ultimate, yet at the same time from another perspective it is relative.

Q. Why do you feel that so many young westerners today look to a Dalai Lama as their most authoritative spiritual symbol and leader? Do you ask yourself that question sometimes?

A. No, I have not given much thought to that. I consider these people as our friends. There are some who show a very close feeling to us for spiritual reasons. But at the same time there are many who are simply human beings showing friendship. I appreciate their friendship greatly.

Q. Yet there are many who feel alienated from their own western religious family. What advice do you give them?

A. Yes. My general advice or suggestion to these people is that it is not necessary to be religious-minded or a religious believer. Even if you remain a non-believer, be a good human being, a warm-hearted person. Kindness and loving-kindess I consider as a universal religion. That's important. I always make a distinction between religious faith and the innate spiritual nature of kindness and human affection. These I consider another form of spiritual value. So you see if these things are there then, for me, there is not much difference whether they take on some religion or not – because the sense of religion is already there. The person may not be called a believer but they are sincerely practising the essence of religion.

Q. Buddhists sometimes say to me that Christianity is a dogmatic religion. Would you agree with that or say that Buddhism is non-dogmatic, even not a religion?

A. Given that I don't have an extensive knowledge of Christianity or the Christian tradition it's very difficult for me to
make a categorical comment on this. But I would personally
think that in almost all the religions we find a difference
between the current religion and the way the original
founder conceived the project. For instance, in the case of
Christianity you have Christ. At his time perhaps dogma did
not have so important a role to play. Then later followers
paid less attention to the reality of the original situation but
took his words as having dogmatic authority. This is the
same in Buddhism – and even in Tibetan Buddhism, for
example, where you find people treating tradition and
custom as more important than the actual source.

But a difference that one could see particularly in Mahayana Buddhism is that we have a very explicit statement from
the Buddha himself that his words are not to be accepted
just out of reverence to himself. Rather they should be tested
and examined only on the basis of one's personal understanding. In that sense there is an explicit liberty given to
the followers of the Buddha. The Buddha made very clear
to his followers the right or liberty to carry investigation even
into Buddha's own words. So, when through investigation
you find some contradiction with actual experience then we
have the right to reject the Buddha. To reject does not mean
totally to dismiss but rather to look for a reason behind the
statement and see why such statements were made even
though they seem to contradict experience.

Q. If you had a young Tibetan as a student and he asked you
to tell who Jesus was what would you say?

A. A great being. There's no doubt. Purely from the Buddhist
viewpoint, of course, Buddhism is considered best for the
Buddhist. This does not mean Buddhism is best for every-

body. Buddhists see Jesus Christ or Mohammed as great beings, great teachers. They taught differently but we would believe that they are either Bodhisattvas or manifestations of Buddha. They apparently seem non-Buddhists but interiorly in their real being they are clearly great enlightened beings. According to Buddhist Scriptures, particularly in Mahayana Buddhism, the final destroyer of Buddha dharma will be a Buddha. There is an understanding in Buddhist tradition that the relevance of Buddha's teaching or its efficacy is limited to time and at a certain point in history it will have lost its effectiveness and then there will be a Buddha who will then close the chapter. A destroyer of the dharma.

Q. Does a meditator or monk living and meditating in solitude help the world?

A. Yes.

Q. How?

A. Like Christians who believe in God or a Creator, Buddhists, who do not believe in God, do believe in higher beings. Buddhas or Bodhisattvas we consider as higher beings. They have a definite influence. Through solitude and deep meditation they increase the spiritual vibration or spiritual energy in the world. As a result of their solitude and meditation, your own spiritual experience is enhanced. We believe that in a way you become so receptive to the forces of these higher beings that you can evoke the powers of these beings through your meditation. This is one way. Another way is that through such meditation some kind of positive atmosphere is automatically created where these people live.

Q. Are some places more sacred than others?

A. Some vibration or energy is created in the places where such deep meditation is practised by these people whatever their religious belief. So we consider these places as sacred for pilgrimage. These areas are actually charged by such people.

So then when other less highly charged people are there they receive this charge.

Q. Do you think Tibet is a place like that?
A. Tibet has less charge now I think than before. Now it has a lot of negative charge! This is not necessarily superstition, I think, because Tibetans also feel this when they return to Tibet. They feel something really empty even though they are visiting the same buildings in the same place.

Q. How urgent is it for the West to help Tibet? How much time is there?
A. It is extremely urgent, I feel. I think if the present situation continues there is another ten years for Tibet.

Q. What is the spiritual message to the world of the tragedy in Tibet?
A. Nonviolence. That the pursuit of a nonviolent path and the way of compassion and of love are spiritual values.

Q. How do you cope with the life of so much travel and daily publicity?
A. I do not give much thought to this or give special attention to publicity. Of course sometimes we do take some care and notice about publicity. But in front of other people I feel just a Buddhist monk. When I remain in my own home or house I am just a Buddhist monk. So there is no difference, no gap. In front of the public I consider myself just a Buddhist monk and at home my thinking, my speaking and my behaviour are the same. So I don't have to make a special effort to cope with public events because there is hardly any gap between my behaviour, speech or thinking in public or private. This makes it all much easier!

*

The wisdom of the Dalai Lama helps us to understand for our-

selves how our own particular path can be followed with reverence and commitment while growing in respect and humility
towards other paths. There is no doubt that a great spring of
his wisdom is his own daily practice of meditation. And though
we find great diversity even in the different ways of meditation we also find, through our own path sincerely practised,
what he calls the essential religion of love and compassion.

At a talk I was giving in Princeton recently a fundamentalist
Christian walked out when I said I could not say that Christ was
not to be found in everyone. After all, Jesus did not identify the
religion of the thirsty man to whom one gives a drink of water
when he said 'When I was thirsty you gave me drink'. The
deep mystery of Christian faith is the mystery of reality: that the
universal and the particular are in total harmony. Isn't this after
all what it means to say that we have the Spirit of God dwelling
within us and that the mind of Christ is ours? So a Buddhist
teaches and practises the great religious truth that we must love
our enemies while the tragedy of Bosnia unfolds each day under
the pretended banners of Christian and Muslim. The light of
God flashes into us from every good heart.

May our daily pilgrimage open our hearts each day more fully
to that light of love.

With much love

Laurence

Laurence Freeman OSB

Letter Six

September 1993

Dearest Friends,

One afternoon during the monastic experience retreat which was held at Niagara, I went to visit the great Falls. Despite all the nearby honkytonk, catering to the busloads of tourists, the Falls preserve an overwhelming purity and majesty. Some religious groups have dedicated it as one of the world's great natural centres of spiritual power. One can only wonder how the original American Indians must have seen and understood it. It is not merely the monumental power of the spectacle or its size, but the total is-ness of the place which serves to humble and centre the spectator – in himself or herself and in a reality greater than the individual self.

If, as we did, you take the little boat called *The Maid of the Mist* on the lake towards the Falls, seeing them now from below rather than from above, you become far less of a spectator. You are infinitely more humbled by the sheer height of the Falls, their miraculously constant flow of pure energy, and perhaps you are even mentally expanded by the ozone. Yet, in the closeness you also feel the essential stillness and silence of this great manifestation of natural power. Because it is natural, because it is simply itself, you feel from it a purity of being which brings us closer to Being itself.

'His invisible attributes, that is to say his everlasting power and deity, have been visible, ever since the world began, to the eye of reason, in the things he has made,' St Paul said (Romans 1:20). And the great contemplative teachers of Christian living have always urged us to read God, as they do, in the book of nature. This is a wise knowing we today urgently need to recover as we rush towards the precipice of our self-inflicted ecological crisis. It is a wisdom that integrates and completes the different ways of knowing with which we have all been created: the knowledge that enters and transforms us through the eye of the body, the eye of the mind and the eye of the heart.

As the *Maid of the Mist* approaches the mighty curtain of the Falls you realise why the little boat is called that. At the centre of the Falls a cloud of fine spray forms into a thick column as the water crashes into the lake and sends the mist upwards to rest even higher than the crest of the Falls hundreds of feet above. It is like both the 'effulgence of the glory of the Lord' and the 'cloud of unknowing'. It is both a manifestation of the central reality and a way of veiling it from us: a way to see and yet know we cannot see God and live. At a critical point the little boat must turn around with its wet and greatly simplified cargo of mere mortals.

Seeing nature as an allegory of heavenly things has lost its fashion and it seems faintly ridiculous or pietistic to press the point. Yet the spiritual tradition we are beginning to recover today – and with which meditation teaches us how to reconnect – requires that we trust the *naïveté* of this kind of knowing. Without it we cannot see beyond the surface meanings of the great scriptures of the world.

Unless this deeper kind of knowing – what Blake called 'Imagination' – is allowed to move in us and guide us as Christians, we cannot move into the deeper faith that brings our knowledge of Jesus to its fullness. In that depth we let go of the consolatory effect of our ideas about Jesus as we prepare to meet his presence in itself. 'Do not think I am overwhelmed by consolations. Far from it!' wrote that tough-minded 'little flower', Thérèse of Lisieux; 'Jesus does not guide me openly: I neither see nor hear him.' Yet she learned to find him by reading 'the book of life in which is contained the science of love'. Seeing God in nature, finding the science of love in the book of

life, are among the great teachings of the contemplative tradition that modern people are learning to drink from today.

As we continued with the retreat at Niagara we reflected
together on three of the major themes of monastic wisdom as
they relate to the daily pilgrimage of meditation which we had
all come together to deepen and strengthen. The goal of the
monastic life is that of all life, the purity of heart which opens
the eye of the heart to see God in one's self, in others, in all
creation. The first of the three themes we thought about was
asceticism.

Asceticism

As we arrived at the retreat house one of the retreatants
remarked that she was surprised to find an elevator in a house
run by religious. Naturally, she did not carry her bags upstairs.
Nor, I am sure, would she have begrudged the old religious
living there the modest comfort it gave them. Yet her remark
revealed the misunderstanding and distortion of asceticism
which has entrenched itself in the Christian mind. Our ecological crisis alone makes it urgent for us, in our modern orgy of
self-indulgence and our exploitation of natural resources, to
recover the true sense of ascesis.

After the end of the Cold War a new polarisation is likely to
form, not between communist and capitalist, or even East and
West or developed and developing, but between those who see
the crisis we face and those who refuse to see. As more of our
cities and countryside are sacrificed to petrol-driven motor cars
and our water supplies and atmosphere become more endan-
gered, the principles of moderation and self-control become
both political and spiritual concerns.

The word 'asceticism' means training, not punishment. When
it is a 'no' to some desire or pleasure it is always a positive no:
a yes to something greater. It should, therefore, be associated
with joy rather than depression or anger. Properly practised it is
an affirmation and enhancement, indeed a liberation of human

nature, not a rejection or subjection of natural energies. If it has often become another '-ism' in the catalogue of human fanaticisms this is because, as something intrinsically healthy and enlightening, it has become hooked into the dark and life-denying side of the psyche. Self-denial can become an addiction and like all addictions it is a reaction to pain and an escape from truth. This is especially easy in relation to our physical and sexual nature and our unconscious. Most vulnerable and easily hooked are the psyche's drives of self-rejection, its fear of love, its guilt at having grown up.

That part of Christianity which encouraged this unhealthy alliance between these darker psychic wounds and asceticism is now bravely confessing its mistakes. A great contemporary Trappist monk and spiritual guide for many today, Fr Thomas Keating, has described how, entering as a novice fifty years ago, he was told to leave his body outside the monastery. He entered a world where the sincere and committed search for contemplation was often tragically over-identified with suffering. Fr Johnston during the seminar amused us by saying how in the old type of Jesuit novitiate you were given a copy of the Bible with a slip of paper indicating the passages novices were not permitted to read.

Negative asceticism is not only petty-minded in its repression of pleasure or knowledge and in its cultivation of suffering. It is also radically unbiblical. It derives from a distortion of early Christian teaching about the body itself. St Paul hymns the body as a sacrament of divine oneness and sees it as a temple of the Holy Spirit. He identifies the community of believers as the Body of Christ: 'Christ's body is yourselves, each of you with a part to play in the whole' (1 Corinthians 12:27 NJB). Like the spiritual masters of the East he recognised the parallel existence of different kinds of body which are closely linked and cannot be separated in this life, the physical and the subtle. And although he taught celibacy as an option, he saw nothing wrong in the sexual instinct in itself (1 Corinthians 7:36).

Where celibacy was often exalted in Christianity as a rejection of the evils of physicality, in the East it was seen as a means of training the body to be a finer instrument for the human being's highest activity of contemplation. Asceticism, like the body and like the natural world in whose planetary body we are implicated, is an instrument rather than a tool. Tools are exploited and discarded. Instruments, such as in music or as with a chisel in the hands of a master carpenter, are loved by those who use them. An instrument becomes part of us, an extension of our being, a unifying means of the highest self-expression. If meditation is our deepest and most valuable ascesis, the mantra is an instrument not a tool, a discipline not a technique.

Although monasticism has had its periods of unhealthy asceticism it is nevertheless the tradition to which we have readiest access to teach us the true use of this instrument today. St Benedict wanted 'nothing harsh or burdensome' in his school of the Lord's service. Discipline was enforced only for the advancement of charity. Of course the devil can quote scripture, Catholic fundamentalists can quote *Gaudium et Spes* and life-denying monastics can quote the Rule of St Benedict. Yet the Benedictine tradition, no more perfect than any other, has a great treasure for Christianity in its elevation of the virtue of moderation. For not only does St Benedict urge moderation in the practice of all forms of asceticism, he reveals with great wisdom that true asceticism is moderation in all things.

What is moderate? Moderation is the fruit of discernment and its own fruits will be compassion, gentleness and tolerance. It is only the unhealthy ascetic who cannot forgive the self-indulgence of others. Benedict learned this from the Desert Fathers' tradition. In many stories the elders exposed the roots of ascetical vanity and pride. They told of the monk who had been a Roman aristocrat and who was condemned by an Egyptian brother, a former shepherd, for sleeping on a bed and eating cooked food while he slept on the floor and ate raw vegetables. The Roman brought his accuser to the enlightenment of tolerance by explaining how by comparison with his former way of life his asceticism was in fact greater than the shepherd's. The shepherd's life-style had hardly changed when he became a monk.

This question of appropriate and relative asceticism is of urgent relevance to us today. The western world stands accused as a minority of the world population for using a disproportionate amount of global resources. Who will teach it to say a positive 'no' to its insatiable demand for energy and consumer goods and services? Whence comes the discernment to say what is moderate for a European or American suburban commuter and what may be merely enough for the hungry peasant in Asia or South America? Unless we have become simple, how can we live simply or enjoy simplicity? How, without meditation, can we reduce desire and expand generosity of spirit?

Part of the answer to all this lies in realising that asceticism involves more than just the restraint of immediate material desires. 'To realize zen one has to pass through the barrier of the patriarchs. Enlightenment always comes after the road to thinking is blocked.' In a different way Christianity also urges the ascesis of the mind. All that can come of compulsive analysis and arguing about words, says the New Testament, is 'jealousy, quarrelling, slander, base suspicions' (1 Timothy 6:4). Yet Christianity has become one of the most divided and contentious of religions. Those who share the same faith engage in bitter rejection of each other over matters such as the ordination of women or of married men. The contemplative disciplines of the church have always helped restrain the human tendency to prefer our attachment to our own views and policies to the truth. Their value to us now has never been greater.

Appropriate asceticism will always be a matter of debate. It is always going to be difficult to decide when a 'no' to our own desires is not a negation of our nature but an affirmation of our full potential. The medieval rabbi who said that we will all be held to account on Judgement Day for every legitimate pleasure which we did not accept, has great wisdom for us. Above all, though, it is by our fruits that we know ourselves. One immediate test of balanced asceticism is whether it produces beauty.

One of the most beautiful courtyards I ever saw was in a slum house of a religious community caring for the sick street-people of Calcutta. But the main test of true and wholesome asceticism must always be love. Without it any discipline is meaningless and indeed counter-productive. Negative asceticism creates bitter and unfeeling human beings. The right kind forms wise and compassionate response to all situations.

The elders asked Abba Poemen, 'If we see a brother dozing off during prayers how should we reprimand him?' The elder was silent a while and then replied, 'For my part, if I see a brother falling asleep, I put his head on my knees and let him rest.'

For John Main the essential ascesis of the Christian life – and ascesis is a element in any spiritual path – is prayer itself. Here we go to the root. And here the meditator discovers, like the sportsman or artist, the love and delight of training in itself. The best musician does not practise just to get results, compete or win acclaim. So in meditation it is delight enough to know we are on the way and that it is a way, so centred and balancing that it teaches us the middle way in everything. It also leads us to the other theme of monastic wisdom that we explored in Niagara, that of discernment.

Discernment

St Anthony of the Desert is reported to have said that 'some have subdued their bodies in asceticism but for lack of discernment they have fallen away from God'. Monasticism is part of the great wisdom tradition of humanity that shows us all how to practise this vital gift of discernment, which St Benedict called the mother of all virtue. Bede Griffiths, who like John Main and Thomas Merton saw modern monasticism recovering its essentially lay state through the mutual sharing of its contemplative riches with others, still thought of monks as the prophetic order within the church. Slightly marginalised, otherwise rather useless to society, and given something of an extralegal fool's licence, the monk and the meditator learn that discernment is the practice of wisdom in the ordinary things of daily life.

The Greek philosophers thought of wisdom as 'a way of life modelled after the Logos which pervades and governs all things'. For the Christian, wisdom became holiness. It was embodied in the Logos-made-flesh who teaches his followers a way of life by sharing his own life in the Spirit with them by direct transmission. In eastern religion great importance is given to the divinised human being or avatar. Such a person is seen as a great window in the wall of space and time through which many others can pass. To know such an enlightened being saves you from the rigorous obligations of law and ritual. It is like finding an express train when you expected one that stopped at every junction. In Christian faith this aperture has become infinitely open for all peoples in the human consciousness of Jesus.

One of the essential means of discernment in the monastic tradition was the master–disciple relationship. Often it meant a turbulent wrestling with the disciple's pride, fear or restlessness. Yet it was not seen as an indoctrination of the student. It was for liberation. Even the discipline of obedience was practised not to break the ego but to open the ear of the spirit to the disciple's own inner voice, his true self and so to his true will. Nowhere is the subtlety of this relationship made clearer in the desert tradition than in the stories that describe a reversal of roles between master and disciple.

All this is implicit in our relationship with Jesus: the same Jesus who washed his disciples' feet – to their consternation – and who called them friends. The monastic tradition of discernment with the help of the master is rooted in the knowledge of God which Jesus promised to share with us without limit, holding nothing back of what he has heard from his Father. It is friendship of the highest degree.

Discernment is also found in scripture, according to the wisdom tradition. This does not mean scholarship or even great mental familiarity with the texts. Many of the desert stories emphasise that much time, patience and humility was needed to discern through the scriptures. Monks who had the ready answer at their fingertips were told to go off and chew the word some more. The desert monks with much labour learned the scriptures by heart. St Pachomius, for example, insisted that all his community learn to read and that they all learn at least the New Testament and Psalms by heart.

The word of God then became literally part of them. It formed and nourished their inner world and, because reading was then practised aloud, it even became part of them in a physical and external way as well. It is very hard for us with so much more superficial and cerebral an approach to the word to imagine how deeply enlightening scripture could become for those who chewed the word so constantly. Yet, if Cassian is to be believed, we can discover this deeper knowing for ourselves through pure prayer. The ascesis of the mantra, he said, leads us to see into the deeper layers of the meaning of the scriptures when at other times we come to read them.

It is above all in prayer itself that the gift of discernment or wisdom is transmitted. St Paul says, indeed, that it is only by the renewal of mind and the transformation of being that occurs when the mind and heart are united in the supreme human act of worship that you 'will be able to discern the will of God, and to know what is good, acceptable and perfect' (Romans 12:2). Perplexed and divided as we are today over so many questions of social morality and with science presenting us with ever more dilemmas as it masters the processes of nature, we need to recover this ancient wisdom. The authority for moral decisions can no longer come from a single external source, legal or religious. It must first resonate with the authority of our own experience, if this has been opened up, if our inward eye has begun to be illumined (Ephesians 1:18).

For this interior awakening, the monastic wisdom teaches, we need experience of the third theme we looked at in the Niagara retreat: solitude.

Solitude

One of the best Christian descriptions of solitude is a passage from St Aelred of Rievaulx's *Spiritual Friendship*. In it he describes an experience he had 'the day before yesterday' while walking around the cloister. He was watching his fellow monks when the consciousness struck him that there was 'none there whom I did not love and by whom I did not feel myself loved. I was filled with a joy that soared beyond the pleasures of this world. I felt my spirit pass out into all and their affection flow back into me . . .'

Where there is love, there is God. Aelred's description of the transforming ecstasy of human love opening us to God goes to the heart of the Christian gospel. It explains why marriage and the home are in no way less of a spiritual path than monasticism or the cloister.

But why should this be a description of solitude? We can see it was an experience that arose from solitude by the way he describes the sense of unique individuality he felt in that moment of agape: 'I was gazing on them as one might admire in paradise the leaves and flowers and fruit of every individual tree.'

Solitude is no more to be identified with isolation or withdrawal than asceticism is to be confused with pain and repression. Solitude is essentially the discovery and acceptance of our uniqueness. It is therefore, as John Main insisted, the necessary basis for all relationship. As long as we relate from what in us is still stereotyped or standardised by convention, our human relationships cannot reach the depth of divine love.

Physical withdrawal, in differing degrees, is necessary for everyone, at times. To practise meditation morning and evening may well be the recommended daily dose of solitude for many people. But its purpose is not to escape from human beings. Solitude rescues us from the unconscious assimilation in the crowd of humanity, the mob, which absorbs and destroys our uniqueness. St Benedict describes the Lord 'seeking his own workman in the multitude of people' and calling 'Who is the one who wants life and longs to see good days?' The person who replies 'I am the one' has begun the pilgrimage from the egotistical mentality of the crowd into the spiritual conscious-ness of the community of men and women who can love each other because they know they are loved.

Some meditators experience the discovery of their uniqueness in a sudden moment of terrifying awareness that they are utterly unique in the universe. At first this seems to mean they are utterly alone. As the experience is integrated, however, and the fruits of meditation begin to appear in ordinary life, they realise that, far from being alone, they are in fact one with all. The word 'monos', which gives us 'monk', does not essentially mean alone but 'one': with ourselves, with others, with creation, with God. Evagrius said that the monk is one who is detached from all and in harmony with all.

Our image of solitude is often negative: withdrawal, isolation, distance from others. But this misrepresents the hermitage which is like a silent, invisible spiritual concourse; a place where many can converge, as in Aelred's cloister, without sinking into a crowd, and become a community of love. Every human heart is a hermitage, if we care to enter and find ourselves there in union with all. In solitude friend, foe and stranger are equally known in love. The best revelation of solitude might be that of being lost in a milling crowd and suddenly hearing your name called by someone you know and knowing yourself recognised. It is the moment in the Gospel where Mary Magdalene is brought to both self-knowledge and the knowledge of the risen Jesus simultaneously by his utterance of her name.

Solitude in the monastic tradition is associated with positive energies released for the good of others. Although it is a way of non-action (the *wu-wei* of Chinese thought), it is not inaction. In the same way nonviolence is not a passive surrender to violence. Every meditator discovers this in the physical and interior stillness of meditation.

In that stillness we learn the language of silence, the 'language of cosmic adoration' as Gandhi called it. Like all languages it is best learned by total immersion. It expresses itself not in the refusal or inability to communicate, but in the liberation from verbal violence, such as slander and gossip, and in the power to communicate the healing word of God.

Of course, as the monastic wisdom teaches us, solitude will bring us to deserts of aridity, distraction and discouragement. These are real tests for which we must be constantly prepared. But they are not to be feared. If we have truly entered solitude, not isolation, then at these times of trial we will find in each other ministers of strength and inspiration.

We need the wisdom of a tradition to support us on the pilgrimage of meditation. We need also to have that tradition incarnated in a real community which can inspire, correct and support us. If we find that this gift is being given to us we will for sheer joy share it with others.

Let us continue to keep each other's journey and growth in our hearts.

With much love

Laurence

Laurence Freeman OSB

Letter Seven

John Main's Anniversary
30 December 1993

⟡

Dearest Friends,

At the end of October I set off on a six-week visit to meditators that led from Canada and the USA to the Philippines, Singapore and Malaysia before returning home to London. The grace of such a pilgrimage is to discover the still point at the centre of so much change and diversity: the Spirit who is one and the same in an infinity of forms. I am taught again and again about the universal simplicity of meditation, the thirst for its wisdom among people in every culture and the grace of the teacher which so many people are finding in John Main.

In the Philippines, after the Manila Conference, I went to Dumaguete where Fr Gerry Pierse has led groups for a number of years and has recently built a meditation room next to his church which was opened by the bishop on the day I arrived. After the retreat I visited a meditation group that meets weekly in the local prison where Fr Gerry is chaplain. The prisoners live in crowded conditions, up to sixty to a cell, and, as in every prison I have visited, it confronted me with the absurd and inhumane reality of the penal system. The twenty-five, or so, meditating prisoners converge in a rough outbuilding off the central courtyard. They sit on benches and, under the leadership of one of their own number, begin with a time of scripture reading and sharing. During the meditation the workshops and other activities of the prison go on as loudly as ever. Afterwards they spoke about how their discipline of the mantra was helping to find meaning in the wreck of their lives and joy in their daily anguish. The greatest obstacle they faced was not, as for so many, the lack of time or motivation, but the ridicule of their fellow-prisoners.

One of the prisoners, with a frightening story of unjust arrest, spoke of the agony of his separation from his young children. Meditation, he said, had opened up an inner freedom which empowered him to face his suffering with hope and a sense of dignity.

In Manila I also visited a drug rehabilitation centre where meditation has recently been introduced into the daily programme. The residents, mostly in their twenties, formed a most remarkable community of great courage and total honesty. Their discipline of recovery is extreme but freely and even joyfully observed. There is a spirit of forgiveness and acceptance. No one is expected to pretend to be better than they are. In the broken fragments of their lives a spirit is acknowledged to be at work, healing and restoring them to a capacity for relationship. No one could meditate with them, or take part in the song and dance entertainment which followed supper, without realising that the power at work among them is love. Through meditation, introduced each morning by one of Fr John's tapes, they have been helped to discover that the source of the love at work between them is to be found within themselves.

Many of those recovering from drugs or alcohol spoke of the feeling of failure and inadequacy which had led them to seek such a desperate escape from reality. The goal they had been set by society or family had often been one of perfection or achievement and their lives had been broken against it. Their new goal – and life must have a goal – was very different. Rather than perfection, their goal had become one of self-acceptance, relationship and wholeness. In other words, their life was deeply and truly religious.

St Gregory of Nyssa said that the 'contemplation of God's face consists in journeying towards God ceaselessly and in moving forward constantly in the endless following of the word'. A meaningful life requires the imagination of a goal. But we need also to remember the goal is never achieved. If that is forgotten or denied, as it so often is by religious people, the divine goal becomes identified with perfection. Where perfection rather than wholeness becomes the goal we are led down one of three roads: arrogance, hypocrisy or breakdown. Of the three, it is brokenness that offers the best chance of being saved.

From the brokenness of our humanity we can learn the healing and transcendent wisdom of self-acceptance and the non-judgemental acceptance of others. Meditation makes more sense to the broken or humbled parts of us than to the well-defended, successful or public poses that form the more assertive parts of our identity. In meditation we learn to forgo judgement and condemnation – the acts and attitudes that fill prisons with people whom society could help in better ways and that also so often scatter broken relationships through our lives. Simple and pure awareness, without judgement or evaluation, such as we practise in meditation, is always compassionate. It is the proof of our essential goodness that if we can cease to judge one another we will naturally love each another.

It is strange the places and relationships where we meet God, the goal of our lives. God who is the 'life of all free beings' can be met more richly in the prisoner who shares the deep despair and hope of his life than in the professional servants of religion. God who is the fullness of being can be found more wholly in the self-exposure of the recovering drug addict than in the performance of religious ritual. This is the constant message of the Bible, of course, but it is astonishing how frequently religion claims the copyright on God.

Thomas Aquinas said that all we can accurately say about God is that God is, not what God is. Because the idea of God that activates our image of God is so powerful in our lives this is a truth that needs always to be restated before religious people make their dogmatic statements about what God wants or does not want us to do. Our highest goal and value in life is God even if we don't use the word itself. The linguistic symbol 'God' functions actively in deciding how we relate to ourselves and others. It also shapes the kind of society and religion we live in. Although, for example, the Christian knows that 'God is spirit', most Christians automatically refer to God as He. If pressed, they might admit that God is not more male than female. yet it is much more unsettling to refer to God as She and it can create violent resistance. The reason is that the male symbol of God plays such a powerful role in upholding our male-dominated power structures and decision-making systems of government both in society and in church. To touch the image of the all-male God is thus to dare to question the validity of a male-dominated church.

If, as the Christian contemplative tradition has always taught, our knowledge of ourselves and our knowledge of God are inseparable, it must be true that our image of God and of ourselves and our society are interwoven as well. When one changes so must the other. And this is the radical shift in religious consciousness happening among us all today.

Most people received an image of God formed collectively by family, church and school – and today more often by the media – which contained powerful forces of fear and guilt. It is a God of power and majesty, a God of the winners and achievers. As every meditator knows, this image of God is directly confronted and gradually dissolved in the work that is silence. Meditation restores us to the dimension of mystery in God which religious dogma and ritual can so easily ignore, despite the fact that the mysteriousness of God whom 'no one has seen or can see' is one of the most fundamental of all biblical assertions about God. God also becomes the One whose power and glory appear not only in success and strength but equally in the down side of human experience. Mother Teresa once said reflectively that she had no trouble understanding the power and glory of God. It was the humility of God that mystified her.

Recovering the reality of the mystery that is God profoundly reshapes our lives. It also restores mystery to those parts of our experience which we had perhaps despaired of or seen as meaningless. As the image of a God who rewards and punishes dissolves we begin instead to see the God of Christian faith 'who is love'. Love, as we know, can appear anywhere at any time and in the most unlikely of human relationships: with a dying stranger, with an old enemy, with someone long familiar we have wrongly taken for granted. Love neither rewards nor punishes. It celebrates with the joyful and grieves with the sorrowful.

This is the God one meets in the inhumanity of prisons or the brokenness of recovering drug addicts. It is not the God one can speak of too readily or state that 'he' wants this or that of us. Strangely, recovering the mystery of God through silence also restores a new glow of meaning to routine language about God in word or ritual. For many Christians or former Christians, meditation reconnects them to the presence of the Spirit to be found in the Bible and sacraments. For us all it restores a sense of the primacy of relationship in human existence. Daily practice teaches the meditator that productivity, affluence or success are not worth the deterioration of personal relationships in family and friendship which they so often cause. Gradually it dawns on us that God is the fundamental relationship of every human existence, and all human relationships are rooted in God and grow from it.

In practical terms, said the desert monks, the goal of meditation is purity of heart. Cleansing the doors of perception, said William Blake, reveals everything as it truly is – infinite. Meditation purifies the heart and frees us from the veil of egotism's fear and desire to see the God who is love.

It is easier to understand what seeing God means if we think there are three ways of perception in human consciousness. The first 'eye' is the physical. It gives most of us the basic data of consciousness, but by itself it cannot perceive meaning. That is the work of the 'eye' of the mind which through its multiple activities of logic and imagination makes sense of what we experience. Both these eyes deal with experience objectively. We 'see' things both with the physical and the mental eye as if they were separate from ourselves. We stand outside and look at.

But the eye of the heart sees differently. According to St Augustine, the 'whole purpose of this life is to restore to health the eye of the heart whereby God may be seen'. Yet God can never be looked at or viewed as an object. We cannot therefore see God with the objective vision of the mind or physical eye, although of course these forms of perception do grant wonderful secondary knowledge of God. What can truly be called the vision of God, however, involves a participatory way of perception. We see God in the Spirit who is God's own self-vision. For the Christian this points to the grace and truth of Jesus sharing his spirit with us, 'the mind of Christ' dwelling in us. Among other things this means we may well be seeing God without knowing that we are. There is no shortage of self-professed agnostics or atheists who have rejected the religious image of God but whose lives and being radiate the vision of God through love and compassion, generosity and humility. They are at least matched in number by religious people who are convinced they know exactly what God is like but who are condemned by their own intolerance and lack of human warmth.

To see God, then, does not mean seeing anything different. It does mean seeing everything differently. Unfortunately we are easily tempted to seek to see things we don't usually see and then to imagine that these altered states of consciousness are the real thing or are at least bringing us closer to God. From Paul in the Acts of the Apostles who called the magician Bar-Jesus a false prophet and 'enemy of true religion', to all the true teachers of East and West, psychic powers and altered states have been dismissed as deviations from the spiritual path. Jesus himself, while possessing miraculous powers, made faith not magic the basis of a disciple's relationship with him. But today, as then, the extraordinary peak experience, or an entertaining description of it, is often more appealing than the ordinary discipline of purifying the heart.

The New Testament does not give us a very schematic

account of the transformation of consciousness which faith in Christ brings about. But transformation there certainly is: St Paul talks about a remaking of your mind and a transformation of your whole nature, an illumination of your inward eyes and a making new in mind and spirit. As this is clearly the result of a process, a new way of life, it must proceed by stages. Perhaps the first stage is that described as the gifts of the Spirit. These include the extraordinary charisms of healing, miraculous powers, prophecy and ecstatic utterance. Not everybody experiences these in the same way or at all, but they represent at the least a break in religious routine. St Paul does not mock or belittle these gifts but he insists they are temporary and that it is the higher gifts we should be aiming for. These gifts, faith, hope and love, last for ever. The greatest of them is love.

After the gifts, the second stage of transformation unfolds with the fruits of the spirit: love, joy, peace, patience, kindness, goodness, fidelity, gentleness and self-control. These qualities reflect permanent changes in human personality and a real transformation of nature. But they are undramatic except to the person in whom the transformation is taking place. When they become evident to others they are unlikely to make the front page of the tabloids. There is a vital quality of the spiritual which does not seem to translate well into the mass media and therefore usually fails to achieve popularity. Even the saints are usually admired for the wrong reasons.

The goal of the process of transformation in Christ, however, is found in the Beatitudes. These are in direct contradiction of most mundane values of wealth, power and fame. They portray a way of seeing human existence that shocks us by its simplicity, vulnerability and innocence. While respected conventionally as great wisdom, the Beatitudes are generally dismissed as naïve, poetic or otherworldly. But their quality is unworldliness, not otherworldliness. Poverty of spirit, gentleness, purity of heart, grieving, the hunger for justice, mercy, peacemaking and martyrdom are disturbing ideas to select as examples of human fulfilment. But we have reached the goal of 'constantly journeying towards God' once we have begun to live from these eternal and therefore divine values.

To see God is not to see anything extraordinary but to see ordinary things as they truly are. Aquinas therefore described contemplation as the simple enjoyment of the truth. Seeing reality as it truly is, is remarkably difficult. We cast onto people and situations around us an infinitely complex web of our own inner assumptions and half-conscious prejudices. Even with others we rarely see further than the egotistical layer of their consciousness, judging them therefore by the degree to which they please or displease us. Even with regard to ourselves we know a person who has been conditioned and shaped by social and psychological forces and we rarely love what we see of ourselves.

Seeing God means seeing others and ourselves as we are and the test will be if we love what we see. The love itself that we experience will be God. That is, we will see God from within the mystery revealing itself in humanity.

Perhaps the true test of the vision of God is that we are able to look steadily at what we usually turn away from in fear or revulsion. Death and dying, sickness, old age and suffering are not easy to behold and it is even less easy to see beauty, goodness and meaning in them. Until we can see God in them we will not be able to see the true nature of God in life, youth, beauty and health. Because these things are so much easier to behold, Jesus pointed out their opposites as the privileged place to find him: 'For when I was hungry, you gave me food; when thirsty, you gave me drink; when I was a stranger you took me into your home, when naked you clothed me, when I was ill you came to my help, when in prison you visited me' (Matthew 25:35f).

In passing on this teaching of Jesus which the Spirit empowers them to do in every generation, Christians are teaching a way of seeing God. Today, in trying to do this, Christianity faces the crisis of all the consequences of its centuries of compromise with the Master's teaching, its institutional self-centredness and its lack of contemplative depth. Yet its message is of vital importance for a world facing the critical consequences of its abandonment of wisdom.

As I travelled from Europe to America and then on to Asia I was struck not only by the wonderful diversity of humanity but also by some of its terrifying samenesses. Among these the greatest is shopping. Everywhere the culture of consumerism has made shopping from a necessity to an entertainment activity and even a way of life. It symbolises the trivialisation of values which separates us from the deeper call of our own nature. Its individualism, competitiveness and envy tend to lock us into egocentric projects of self-fulfilment which are doomed to disappointment by their own hollowness. How, I wondered, does Christianity, supposedly the religion of the western world from which this culture is generated, address the problem?

For the young in particular Christianity is identified with the church and the church is viewed as a denier of pleasure. Its true role as a teacher of meaning seems to them to have been supplanted by that of judge and moralist. It is not to the church on the whole that people turn who are seeking the meaning of the 'true self' that Jesus said is worth more than the world and all its consumer goods.

Perhaps this will change when Christianity has achieved the transition from a medieval form to a modern form which was begun with the Second Vatican Council. Then, with a courage no other religious body has shown, the Catholic Church turned away from its self-induced isolation and obsession with perfection and turned to find the Lord in the modern world by reading the signs of the times. It sought out its own roots and the Spirit was released in a rich diversity of social and spiritual movements. The current reaction against this force of renewal is perhaps a natural phase in the process of any revolution.

But it can be no more than a temporary slowing down of the Spirit. Among all the meditators I visited I was inspired by the growth, in depth and in openness, as well as by the way the weekly meditation groups are expanding. In Montreal it was heartening to see the spread of the teaching of meditation among the majority French milieu, something which has happened widely only since the Priory closed and we moved the International Centre back to London. In Ottawa and Florida national retreats were held for meditators across Canada and the USA. Meditation group leaders often introduce themselves at such meetings as coming from a 'very small group' as if that were something to be apologetic about. In many ways the smaller the group the greater its strength of faith and so the more powerful the spiritual energy it shares with its members and all around it.

'The hope for the salvation of the world', says the Book of Wisdom, 'lies in the greatest number of wise people.' But perhaps the best schools of wisdom are those with small numbers. Certainly I felt that these small but ever-growing communities of meditation were contributing to the renewal of Christianity and bringing more wise people into the world. They understand the urgent need for wisdom in every part of the world and the necessity for conditions of harmony and peace if human life is to achieve its goal and fulfilment. St Augustine said that the whole purpose of life is to open the eye of the heart. St Irenaeus says the same when he said that the glory of God is a human being fully alive and the life of a human being is the vision of God.

The community of meditators around the world, with all their non-Christian brothers and sisters, are living out the truth of these early teachers of the church. The deepening of prayer in Christianity thus renews the church as a prophetic force on earth. It is interesting that three of the greatest modern teachers of this spiritual deepening – Thomas Merton, John Main, Bede Griffiths – should have been monks. They were able to draw directly on the spiritual wisdom of the desert tradition of primitive lay monasticism which predates the medieval period at which much monasticism and other aspects of Christianity are often arrested.

When Christians meditate they not only return to their

spiritual roots but advance the renewal of the church into its new forms and ways of being for the world. The impulse to pray, as the early monks well knew, is an elemental urge in human nature: to return to our source and to attain our goal. But it also requires continuous renewal and perseverance. Our fragility and inconstancy are obvious human weaknesses. Not so obviously, though, they are also crucibles of the power of divine love.

I felt a powerful bond of love to be growing among the meditators, groups and Centres in our Community which strengthens us all in the 'endless following of the word'. Let us hope we can continue to receive that grace as well as share it generously with others.

With much love

Laurence

Laurence Freeman OSB

Letter Eight

Feast of the Holy Trinity
29 May 1994

My Dearest Friends,

In his *Journal of a Soul* Pope John XIII tells of a particularly intense period of anxiety he was once passing through. Night after night he would wake in the early hours of the morning, tossing and turning with concern for all the problems of the church. Eventually he would slip back to sleep with the comforting thought 'tomorrow I will talk about all this with the pope'. Then he would open wide his eyes, fully awake, remembering that now he was the pope.

The story delights, I think, because it reminds us of the human holiness even of a pope and especially of this pope's amused humility at his own humanity. But it is also a story that teaches us something. With a light touch it uncovers the deepest question of identity in the human mind. 'Who am I?' – the basic self-enquiry which was Ramana Maharshi's way of pursuing the true self to its source – lies our whole life long waiting to be resolved one day. Even if we dismiss it as meaningless, self-centred or silly there will be moments, in the early hours of the morning or at the hour of death, when this question will remind us that it is there. Embedded in the silent ground of consciousness this non-verbal question and our response to it shape and define the kind of life we live.

It is a disturbing question. However many problems life may hold, the certainty about our identity offers hope that they can be resolved or endured. Without identity, however, where is existence, the most basic of all human possessions? Most of the time we readily prefer existence with problems rather than no existence at all. But if we cannot be certain about our true identity then nothing is certain.

Oliver Sacks' book *The Man who Mistook his Wife for a Hat* described with pathos and humour how the tiny neurological and brain misfunctions, the equivalent of loose screws or electrical shorts, utterly confound identity and the powers of ordinary perception that we take so much for granted. Recently I went to visit an aunt of mine suffering from Alzheimer's; or rather, whose children were suffering from her apparent absence of mind, as she had reached a stage of the disease where she seemed sublimely contented. In that strange absence and non-recognition there was nevertheless a sense of presence and identity. Most of the normal rational and linguistic channels of communication were down, as with the mentally handicapped, but as with them also there was a presence of love and unreserved gentleness.

Illness and dying, like the pope's confusion in the early hours of the morning of who he was, press home our modern anxiety about identity. This, like the terror of meaninglessness and the absence of any relish for life, occupy most of the psychologist's fifty-minute hour in offices and clinics around the world. We deal very inadequately with the question of 'Who am I?' when we reply with a name, nationality, work-occupation or family role. Even less adequately with the proliferation of credit and identity cards carried in our wallets or handbags. The hour will come when we will be forced to acknowledge the tenuousness and mortality of these identities and, in letting them go, to travel deeper into the ground of being to find our true self. Speaking of this search for true selfhood, Jesus described it not only as the greatest of all values but as the source of value.

Meditation is the way we engage with this fundamental value. In meditating we cease to evade the overwhelming question of 'Who am I?' And so we learn to live with greater wisdom the relative realities of our different ego-roles. Discretion, which was for St Benedict the mother of virtue, is the capacity to discern the distinctions between these roles and the true self, between the temporal and the eternal, the real and the unreal, and to see how subtly they interweave in the human drama. When we sit to meditate at the beginning and end of each day's activities and problems we go straight for the truth which so often gets lost or trampled as we act out our roles and beliefs. The truth is simply the reality of our eternal identity; or its unreality, as the Buddhists would say. Perhaps there is not so great a difference, at the silent end of the line, between what some call the Self and others the non-Self. Certainly any image or definition of what the true self means is untrue to its reality.

> Of course we all 'have knowledge', as you say. This 'knowledge' breeds conceit; it is love that builds. If anyone fancies that he knows, he knows nothing yet, in the true sense of knowing. But if anyone loves, he is acknowledged by God.
> (1 Corinthians 8:1–3)

This primal strand of Christian theology – the apophatic or unknowing way of knowing – was developed long before the great western divide between theology and contemplation took place; and long before theology was subordinated to the needs of the institutional church for uniformity and orthodoxy. The cold and condemning term 'heretic', applied damningly to Jesus, himself accused by his religious judges as a 'blasphemer', essentially means 'one able to choose'. As such it enshrines the absolute necessity of human freedom in the search for God. Only free beings can respond to God's invitation to know, love and serve him. Anything less could only bore God. Human relationships give us some clue as to the mind of God because they show us how fear and unfreedom prevent love from reaching its fulfilment and frustrate our need for union.

Naturally, we may choose wrongly, just as we can forget who we are while half asleep. But, as St John says, the great power of correction is not punishment or the fear of punishment, but love in the form of unconditional forgiveness. This is translated into social and political action as non-violence. Forgiveness and non-violence threaten the identities of institutions quite as radically as 'Who am I?' disturbs the ego's *status quo*. By releasing self-knowledge and the power of love, meditation makes a great difference to the way we live personal relationships as well as to the way religious and social institutions behave. The capacity of meditation to reform attitudes and open consciousness shows how urgent it is for Christianity to recover the wisdom of unknowing.

Pope John would probably have enjoyed the story of a Sufi master who went to cash a cheque at a bank. The cashier asked him to identify himself, at which the Sufi took a mirror out of his pocket, looked into it and said, 'Yes, it's me all right.'

Our true identity is self-evident and self-authenticating. It does not, like the many ego-identities, depend upon the approval or recognition of others. Yet even the self-realised person trying to cash a cheque without proof of identity will have trouble convincing the cashier to trust him. As the trials of Jesus show, the knowledge of the true self is not translatable into ways of understanding that are based only on knowing and that reject unknowing. 'My kingdom is not of this world.' Hence the struggle, in church and society down the centuries, between prophet and administrator.

Knowledge of the true self is the basis of the prophet's testimony. It explains the authority of Jesus who 'knew where he came from and where he was going' and who therefore could claim to know the Father. It is a knowledge which the New Testament frequently describes as a kind of vision even though it does not concern itself with visions or locutions. St Paul (2 Corinthians 3:18) says that it is a vision enjoyed because a 'veil' of ignorance has been removed to let us see the glory of God 'as in a mirror'.

He does not specify where or what this mirror is but the greatest commentators have always understood it to be the human heart. It is the heart which St Paul also says is the point where the Spirit of God enters and fills human consciousness: where Christ prays in us. Because the heart is this point of intersection between creator and creation it has not been limited to one place. It is nowhere and everywhere. This is also what the *Cloud of Unknowing* says of the work of meditation.

The heart is a kind of magic mirror because by looking into it we see not an image but reality itself. And we are transformed, Paul says, by seeing into what we see. Contemplation divinises. St John, with his love of the imagery of light and vision, affirms the same truth when he says that although we do not know what we will be like 'when Christ appears', we do know – we will be like him because we shall see him as he is (1 John 3:2). He then says that this hope is the reason why we purify ourselves. For him as for the early Christian writers 'purity' was primarily understood not in terms of moral behaviour but of spiritual vision – enlightenment, as we would say today.

This came from the master himself, who said that the pure of heart can see God. For those early followers of the Way, the vision of God was the commanding purpose of their life. 'The whole purpose of this life ... is to restore to health the eye of the heart whereby God may be seen,' said St Augustine. For the early monks purity of heart was the immediate goal of all their labours. And for their successors today, among them those of us who practise the 'pure prayer' they taught, it is the purpose of the mantra.

The doctrine of the vision of God has inspired Christians down the centuries. But it has often been rendered crudely literal, vision being interpreted as physical or mental rather than spiritual, purity as exclusively moral, not perceptual. It is necessary to soak the active mind in scripture to ensure that the true meaning of these crucial terms of Christian life and prayer do not become hijacked by fundamentalism or legalism. The most penetrating vision of the divine expressed in human terms is described in the Beatitudes. They do not list rules of behaviour or legal canons. They portray attitudes, orientations and ways of response. Even though they confound our expectations and overturn worldly wisdom they speak an incontrovertible truth and are therefore liberating.

No one seeking God is unaware that discipline and self-control are also necessary at every level of physical and mental consciousness if the heart is to be purified and the vision of God unveiled. The purpose of discipline is not to restrict but to liberate. So, the emphasis of Jesus and the New Testament falls not on regulation and moral restriction but on liberty of spirit and faith. This is the new 'Law' of Christianity replacing the legalism of religious regulations and prohibitions which so readily become the breeding ground of scrupulosity, hypocrisy, guilt, judgementalism, infantilism, co-dependency, pride and coldness of heart. The most dangerous people are the unalive who obey the rules with no understanding of why they do so. In his great chapter 7 of the letter to the Romans, St Paul proclaims the Christian transcendence of this kind of legalism:

> You . . . through the body of Christ have become dead to the Law and so you are able to belong to someone else, that is, to him who was raised from the dead to make us live fruitfully for God. (Romans 7:4 NJB)

If the Law he refers to is merely the deuteronomic regulations there is nothing very startling in this. But if it is the principle of religious legalism itself that is being discarded then the biblical tradition has transcended its cultural origins through Jesus. And Christianity has therefore become truly universal. What is more, we can see, in this great Pauline cry of freedom and vision, the startling discovery of the meaning of humanity to God – that we may bear fruit for God. Jesus first makes this point in St John's Gospel (15:8) when he says that his Father is glorified by our 'bringing forth very much fruit'. For those who have eyes to see and ears to hear there is a secret of the universe being revealed.

Jesus fills out this mystery many times by depicting God not only as the 'One who truly is' but as the 'One who really cares'. For Jesus and so for us, God is not merely a transcendent being, the unmoved Mover, but one who lives and feels from within the full range of human experience. If God is the source of human consciousness why should the divine nature not know fully what it is to be human? The capacity of God to care for the greatest and the slightest human feeling provides Jesus with one of his most moving parables on prayer. In the Gospel of Luke (Ch. 11) Jesus says that if you had a friend who woke you up in the early hours asking for some bread, you might first tell him to get lost, but eventually the 'very shamelessness' of the request would make you get up and give him all he needs. 'And so I say to you, ask and you will receive; seek and you will find; knock and the door will be opened.'

This is the great assurance that we are not wasting our time in prayer. And we are not wasting God's time. It assures us that meditation is valuable to us because it is also of value to God. And it has meaning to God because love cares. Our daily needs and hurts matter – ultimately – just as the deeper lifelong processes of healing and liberation from fear that unfold in us are significant. Jesus chose a simple, childlike story to express this most human secret of the universe. It conveys the mystery subtly and delicately.

But precisely because of its subtlety it can easily be misinterpreted. The assurance that prayer is 'heard' can, perhaps through our desperation or through our superstition and greed, be reduced to mere materialism and magic. Prayer then becomes no more than the satisfaction of desires rather than the fulfilment of our nature and the ultimate meeting of our needs. The understated humour of the story is the key to its simple, profound meaning – the shameless effrontery of the cry for help ensures that it will be heard.

There is a kind of shamelessness in meditation. The *Cloud of Unknowing* frequently speaks of it as a nakedness before God. And the mantra is a kind of steady, constant knocking on the door of the heart. To see this, like seeing the humour in our own 'shamelessness', lifts the heavy, neurotic burden of solemnity from our spirituality and off our relationship to God. The cold humourlessness of religious legalism means we can never be humble because, unlike good Pope John, we can never laugh at ourselves. What cannot be laughed at becomes a devil.

The essence of prayer lies a long way from our usual egocentric view of the world and yet prayer has a lot to do with our day-to-day egotism. The fruits of meditation are a progressive liberation from egotism. They teach us that prayer does not essentially consist in our asking for things but in placing ourselves, including our daily needs and wounds, in the presence of God, into the lovingly parental hands of God.

Meditation in this Christian perspective is an act of trust and surrender. It is empowered by the core Christian intuition that our spiritual journey matters deeply, ultimately, not only to ourselves but to God to whom we are travelling. Our act of surrender, then, does not diminish us. Only partial surrenders humiliate. The all-trusting surrender of egotism in the shamelessness of meditation leaves us not less dignified but more humble, more real; and more at peace with ourselves because we are more at one with our true selves.

What we see in these different strands of Christian prayer is the close connection between contemplation, the deepest meaning of human liberty, the vision of God and the true purpose of religion. These ancient themes need to be reviewed and rediscovered in every generation and in every individual's experience. Today this is happening in an unprecedented way because we live in a society where these values have lost their centrality and even their relevance for so many.

It is a situation which was prophetically seen by Cardinal Newman in 1873 when he preached at the opening of a new seminary in England. He said that the church, which had often faced persecution in its history, now faced the greater enemy of a 'irreligious society', where reason had supplanted faith and an epidemic of infidelity had started. His response to infidelity is illuminating. Firstly, he said, there must be an 'elevation of mind, a spirit of seriousness or recollection, a habit of feeling we are in God's presence'. Secondly, sound theology.

Newman's perception about the centrality of the contempla-

tive experience – his words are a good description of mindfulness – anticipated the conviction of twentieth-century Christian
teachers like Karl Rahner, John Main and Bede Griffiths. The
church's response to the spiritual needs of people today must
be mystical rather than dogmatic. More than a century ago
Newman, one of the great and holy theologians of modern
Christianity, saw seminaries primarily as places of training in
contemplation rather than just colleges of orthodox theology.

His description of contemplative awareness finds a deep resonance in the spiritual climate of the late twentieth century.
Our conventional ideas about God and the way we, often
unconsciously, imagine 'Him' must be disturbed by this 'habit
of feeling we are in God's presence'. When you are really with
someone your ideas about them suffer a great change. The
childhood images of God form the earliest layer of our ideas
about God because we think first in images; ideas come later.
These earliest images of God are often associated with feelings
of fear, punishment and of distant authority.

One effect of this is to keep our relationship with God limited
to an egocentric range of knowledge – we see God in terms of
ourselves rather than ourselves in the light of God. Therefore
we speak of God testing us, rewarding us, punishing us for our
good or bad deeds. We live from the child's conviction that we
must be loved exclusively. Only slowly do we accept that we are
loved not exclusively but universally and yet, as the gospel
reveals, uniquely.

Contemplative life needs to be nourished by times of deep
immersion in the true and life-giving images of God found in
scripture. These engage and counteract on their own level the
cultish and egotistic images of God that can distort or pervert
revelation. Undeniably, there have been blasphemous ideas of
God proclaimed by religious institutions – the blessing of
weapons of war or the torture of heretics in God's name. But
even this should not prevent us from embracing the full and
unique Christian insight into the personal nature of the
Godhead.

This is the God who, Jesus says, cares for every human being equally, 'good and bad alike', who is prodigal in love to prodigal sons and daughters, whose grace abounds where sin is found, who turned divinity inside out in order to identify wholly with the humanity and creation with whom he fell in love. This is a crucially important image of God to remember. But with this remembering there must be a wholehearted forgetting of all images. For the presence to become fully conscious there must be an absence to enter. As Anthony Bloom wrote, 'The day when God is absent, when he is silent, that is the beginning of prayer.'

Meditation is a way of self-transcendence and self-knowledge. It unites absence and presence just as it resolves all dualities, all oppositions. Meditation therefore realises what India has long called *advaita*, the realm of unity and non-duality, and what Christian tradition, following Jesus, calls the Spirit. Through the unknowing of deep prayer we know, through the mind of Christ, that, just as for Jesus, 'the Father is greater than I' and yet 'the Father and I are one'. Letting go of our images of a personal God does not therefore mean that we abandon the God who cares, the God who is love. Quite the reverse. Letting go purifies the eye of the heart and empowers us with the vision of God. But it teaches us, too, that we see God only because we are seen by God. And if we become what we see, so does God. God became human so that humanity might become God, was the insight of the Fathers of the church.

Meditation is a way of encountering and knowing God because, as Christian masters have always taught, to know the Self in ourself is to know God who is all in all. To let go of images of ourselves is to stop thinking of ourselves. To let go of images of God is to enter the mystery of God, all thought and speech about whom must begin in and return to silence. The consequence of this daily discipline of pure prayer is not that fewer things image God but that more and more things do.

The few images of God to which we have restricted the biblical tradition – judge, king, creator – become refreshingly expanded. The Bible itself speaks to us of God in many other human aspects: as a dairymaid, farmer, laundress, construction worker, potter, fisherman, midwife, merchant, physician, baker-woman, teacher, writer, artist, nurse, metalworker, home-maker, as well as in images of nature such as that of lion, rock, hovering mother bird, angry mother bear, mother hen, light, cloud, fire and water. Elizabeth Johnson, with her sense of the feminine in divinity, has recognised these images of God in the Bible. Meditation, by restoring health to the eye of the heart, opens us further to see God in everything, in the book of nature. What are the many modern wonders of science and art, great and ordinary, which could expand the biblical repertoire of manifestations of God today?

We could say much more and still fall short ... To put it concisely, 'God is all' (Sirach 43:27).

The rich, explosive diversity of creation is given meaning by its essential unity and simplicity. Meditation saves the diversity of life-forms from becoming distraction just as it saves religion from imprisoning unity in uniformity.

With much love

Laurence

Laurence Freeman OSB

Letter Nine

October 1994

Dearest Friends,

> O, Wonder!
> How many goodly creatures are there here!
> How beauteous mankind is! O brave new world,
> That has such people in't!
>
> (*The Tempest*)

On the morning of the first full day of the John Main Seminar, His Holiness the Dalai Lama entered a hall full of people representing more than thirty countries and two of the world's great religious traditions. He walked bowing low, looking at the people over his hands joined in homage to them, beaming goodwill and humour, noticing those he knew and making everyone feel that he knew them also. The previous evening at the opening of the Seminar, and again early that morning, he had meditated for half an hour in silence with everyone in the hall. So we were already enjoying that goodly and beauteous feeling of shared humanity which meditation creates as it dissolves the barriers of pride and suspicion and separateness. A sense of wonder was already in the air.

But also, I must admit, a certain trepidation. The Dalai Lama had accepted our invitation to lead the Seminar because he remembered so warmly his meeting with John Main in 1980 when they had meditated and eaten together and then shared their vision of the spiritual needs of the modern world. He had also accepted my suggestion that he comment on a number of gospel texts which we had selected and discussed at earlier meetings. From the beginning he reminded us that he was not very well acquainted with Christian scriptures or theology but was ready to read the texts and respond to them 'as a simple Buddhist monk'.

There was no doubt that what he would say would be stimulating. The Dalai Lama's philosophical training from childhood has formed him as one of the most incisive and discerning religious minds in the world. And even if he was to say nothing, any meditator could have sensed the grace of his presence and the powerful radiance of his personal human integration: his holiness. We knew that the benefit of meditating with him opened an experience of clarity and depth, a fuller degree of centred attention, peace and mindfulness which was to make the Seminar a moment of spiritual advancement for us all as individuals, whatever meaning it might have for a wider audience in the future.

Yet, that first morning, we did not know quite what to expect as the Dalai Lama took his seat centre-stage between his Buddhist monk-translator and myself. He turned his attention to the first text, from Jesus' Sermon on the Mount (Matthew 5:38–48). Leaning over it and following each line with his finger he began slowly and carefully to pronounce the words. He spoke the words of Jesus in the midst of a profoundly wakeful, historical silence.

Like every moment of great meaning in life this moment had an almost absurd, deeply disturbing simplicity. Like a child experiencing wonder. Like Miranda, in *The Tempest*, seeing human beings for the first time. This was a moment when the critical, objectifying, judgemental mind was gentle and quietened by something of unquestionable truth, innocence and integrity.

Of course it is impossible to communicate this. Speaking of something 'unquestionable' makes one want to question it! Afterwards speaking with so many who said disarmingly how their eyes had filled with tears as he read the gospel, I felt glad that there were 400 others present to confirm what I felt sitting beside him. The videos and tapes of the Seminar have captured something of this moment and the even stronger moments of understanding and communion for which it opened the door. Either way, I feel certain that the fruits of this John Main Seminar will be real and palpable in many spiritual paths and in the relationship between Buddhism and Christianity far into the future.

The spiritual experience and its fruitfulness testify both to the scriptures and to the person who was commenting on them. For Christians, as for those of other faiths, their scriptures are called 'holy'. Christ as the incarnate Word is present in the words in a direct way. In the fifth century St Caesarius of Arles had a question for his brothers and sisters, 'Which do you think more important, the Word of God or the Body of Christ (in the Eucharist)?' His reply was that they possess equal importance. 'How careful we are, when the Body of Christ is distributed to us, not to let any bit of it fall to the ground from our hand! But we should be just as careful not to let slip from our hearts the Word of God' by listening to it negligently.

The words that carry the presence of the Word are nevertheless subject to human understanding – and misunderstanding. The words of Jesus, in particular, exist for us only in translation and so from the beginning they needed to be interpreted through the mind if the heart was to know their meaning. No religious tradition has refined the instruments of the mind for the perception of truth more carefully than Buddhism. And of Buddhist teachers no one is better trained in this art of perception than the present Dalai Lama.

So as Christians we looked forward to seeing our scriptures, with which we were familiar (and often so familiar that we read them negligently) in a fresh and new way through the Dalai Lama's eyes. To see the Word in the words is, of course, not a merely mental perception. True insight (*vipassana*, in Sanskrit) involves our entire consciousness and forms in us an experience beyond the perceptual range of thought, word and image.

Thomas Aquinas reminds us of this when he says that it is not in propositions or ideas that we put our faith but in the reality which words point to. Meditation, for John Main, was precisely that art of prayerful attention to the truth which leads to the experience of reality which is beyond words, but which also inhabits the worlds of words.

Each day of the Seminar we meditated with the Dalai Lama three times. This not only created an atmosphere of trust and communion; it also regularly cleansed the doors of perception and allowed the Word to shine in silence through the commentary and discussion. Silence and presence were the heart of the Seminar.

The Word of God, then, had its own power and dynamic. We felt it 'alive and active ... [cutting] more keenly than any two-edged sword, piercing as far as the place where life and spirit, joints and marrow, divide. It sifts the purposes and thoughts of the heart. There is nothing in creation that can hide from him' (Hebrews 4:12–13).

But the Word, as St Augustine once said of John the Baptist's role, needs a voice to carry it. For three days the Dalai Lama was that medium, for Buddhists and Christians alike. His presence and personality communicated the Word that yet must always speak for itself.

One should say, perhaps, that Tenzin Gyatso (the present, 14th Dalai Lama) was that medium because it was not his office but his personal humanity that bore authority. More than mere official status, he embodied the rich tradition of Tibetan Buddhism. He was also present to us through an exemplary humanity which had suffered deeply, lost home and country, witnessed and daily felt the ravaging of his people and religion while the rest of the world denied or ignored it; yet he radiated joy and humour in an eloquent absence of all religious pretentiousness or impersonal formality. And above all, he taught the doctrine of love of one's enemies with the authority of one who lived his teaching each day of his life and believed with his whole being in the way of nonviolence. It was not surprising, then, that when he spoke the words of the Sermon on the Mount, 'But what I tell you is this: Love your enemies and pray for your persecutors; only so can you be children of your heavenly Father, who makes his sun rise on good and bad alike . . .', their power and meaning flowed from him into his listeners.

Because of this strange and beauteous freshness of meaning in familiar words spoken in this way, the questions a Christian would naturally want a Dalai Lama to answer – what does 'heavenly father' mean to you? how do you understand Jesus? and so on – acquired a more than casual interest. The answers to these questions by someone who communicated the meaning of the words of Jesus so powerfully would have great importance to any person of faith.

In most discussions there are people quick to swoop down on points of difference and drive wedges between people as they approach each other. Much of our public discourse today is driven by the attitude that people are naturally untruthful and that all feelings of unity or friendship are deceptive. It was a sign of the Holy Spirit at our meeting with the Dalai Lama that our questions and discussions with him were not undermined in this way. There was time for trust and respect to build up to a sufficient degree to allow real understanding to occur.

This was also due to the Dalai Lama's own clarity of purpose in reading the Gospels with us, a purpose which was a model of how dialogue should be held. He began by explaining his limited knowledge of Christianity; he looked forward to learning more about it and, of course, he was commenting on the Gospels simply as a Buddhist. He went on to say that he did not want to cast seeds of doubt in anyone's mind or create confusion. He then repeated his belief that naturally a person should not or need not change their religion, though respecting a person's freedom to do so. Nor did he believe in the eventual merging of all religions into a single 'global religion'. But the common purpose of every religion is to create 'good and happy people' and the true witness of every religion is a 'good heart' full of compassion and tolerance.

No religious leader in the West has convinced as wide a range of people of the value of religion as has the Dalai Lama in his visits to Europe and America, since his exile from Tibet. The media, education, science, entertainment and politics generally combine to disempower religion by marginalising, scandalising or trivialising it. But in a unique way the Dalai Lama, speaking with faith but without dogmatism, with passion and reason, conviction and tolerance of other views, has become a model of authentic religion to a sceptical and materialistic world.

His clarity about the true fundamentals of religion dispels fundamentalism. In the Sermon on the Mount he saw the fundamental law of compassion. And, he asked, quoting Shantideva, 'If you can't show compassion to your enemies, who can you show it to?' Nonviolence is not a passive response to violence but an actively compassionate one. It is the mark of a Bodhisattva in Mahayana Buddhism, who is an enlightened being who chooses to remain in the world for the well-being and liberation of others. In such a person – and the Dalai Lama clearly recognised this in Jesus – you can see that equanimity is the precondition for compassion.

From the clear vision created by inner equanimity one recognises that no human being is irrelevant to one's self, that one's enemies are capable of being one's special spiritual teachers and that the aim of all spiritual practice must be to enhance our capacity for compassion. By remaining in the equipoise of loving-kindness, shown to friends and enemies alike, one is then absorbed into a state of uninterrupted compassion. 'There must be no limit to your goodness, as your heavenly Father's goodness knows no bounds,' Jesus says.

At the ethical level the parallels between Christianity and Buddhism run close and frequently converge. At other levels, which were raised by other gospel passages, the resonance between the beliefs of the two traditions sounded from a depth beyond verbal definition. Thus, the Dalai Lama said, the differences are as important as the similarities. His reading of the Beatitudes perceived the law of causality (karma) in the way

Jesus described the connection between right attitudes and behaviour with 'rewards' such as the vision of God, inheriting the earth, and the kingdom of God. But these, at least conceptually, cannot be directly translated into Buddhist terms. You cannot, as the Dalai Lama quoted a Tibetan saying, put a yak's head on a sheep's body.

Nor did anyone think the experiment worth trying. The Dalai Lama's respect for the Christian belief in a Creator-God was sincere and in no way condescending. And Christians respected the non-theism of the Dalai Lama's vision of reality. On this occasion both Christians and Buddhists, with the open-mindedness that comes with sincere respect for others, learned the deeper meanings of their own beliefs. After discussing the Christian idea of God in the contemplative tradition and hearing of the doctrine of the Trinity, the Dalai Lama was asked by Sr Eileen O'Hea, one of the panellists, what he would like to ask Jesus if he had the chance. He replied quickly, with a laugh, 'What is the nature of the Father?'

The Dalai Lama had shown great courage and trust in agreeing to comment on the Gospels with us. As the Seminar progressed and the meeting of mind and heart deepened in the Word, I realised too, seeing the strength of his mind and insight, what an act of trust it had been on the Christian side to entrust these precious texts to him. It was a trust richly rewarded because of the delicacy with which he used his strength and how he balanced the perceptions of convergence, parallels and resonances between Buddhist and Christian beliefs. This delicacy of strength became clearest in his comments on those passages in which the person of Jesus was central.

About Jesus the Dalai Lama had as many questions about what Christians believed as statements of how Buddhists can see him. Some passages showed Jesus as a teacher (Mark 3:31–5: 'Whoever does the will of God is my brother, my sister, my mother'; Mark 4:26–34: 'The kingdom of God is like this . . .'). Watching and hearing the Dalai Lama read and expound them one realised that a teacher exists in the very act of teaching.

The term 'teacher' denotes a relationship with those willing to be taught according to their different degrees of receptivity. One realised too that Jesus, like any teacher, spoke in the words and metaphors his listeners would best understand. The 'will of God', the 'kingdom of God', intimate relationship with Christ, became once again, through the Dalai Lama's eyes, charged with meaning and wonder.

Even on the question of the Christian mission (Luke 9:2–6) the Dalai Lama's comments opened a deeper and more helpful Christian understanding. He distinguished between the call to mission and the attempt to convert others to our own beliefs. To share the good news or the dharma freely and widely is integral to the faith of any practitioner, Buddhist or Christian. What we share essentially is our practice, through the teaching of the scriptures as well as through one's own degree of realisation. The way to do so is, as Jesus shows in the instructions to his disciples, basically simple and modest. His instruction to them to preach and heal shows also that these are two aspects of one act of service. To share the good news is to heal the many forms of sickness that human nature can be crippled by.

'Jesus declared publicly: "Whoever believes in me, believes not in me but in the one who sent me" ' (John 12:44–50 NJB). The closer we approached the heart of Christian faith, the personal nature of Jesus and his relationship to God, the deeper was the Dalai Lama's focus on the words and his reverence for their meaning. 'Whoever sees interdependence sees the Dharma and whoever sees the Dharma sees the Buddha', he quoted musingly after reading what Jesus in St John's Gospel says of himself.

Vision at this level of perception is, for Christian and Buddhist alike, neither physical nor intellectual. In Jesus' use of the symbol of light the Dalai Lama found a familiar term to describe the wisdom and knowledge which the Buddhist pursues. Faith in Jesus evoked a characteristically analytical Buddhist response describing the need for faith and then the three forms of faith (admiration, aspiration and conviction). Where the darkness of ignorance is dispelled there is salvation.

In the last passage on the Resurrection appearance to Mary
Magdalene the Dalai Lama's commentary made sensible to us
all the mystery of connection that is to be found in the spacious
silence between our many words and ideas. It was not (as for
many westerners) a matter for him of believing or not, but
of how to understand the truth expressed in the Resurrection
narratives. He spoke of the different forms of the body and of
the dharma and he asked us what Christians understood by this
truth. In his way of asking that last question, many of us felt
that he taught us as much as he had given during the whole
Seminar.

After the Seminar about sixty-five meditation group leaders
from many different countries made a three-day retreat
together. As we reflected on the experience we had just shared
with the Dalai Lama, it was clear to me that one valid and
frequently expressed way of describing our experience would
be that we had seen Christ in him.

Certainly we had felt the presence of the Holy Spirit whose
work it is to reveal Christ. And as we were all gathered there
'in his name', was it so surprising that we should have seen
him? 'Here I stand knocking at the door; if anyone hears my
voice and opens the door, I will come in and sit down to supper
with him and he with me' (Revelation 3:20).

Gerard Manley Hopkins wrote in a poem that 'Christ dances
in a thousand places'. Hopkins had seen Christ in a thousand
places which had inspired his poetry but did not carry the overt
religious symbolism or the *imprimatur* of 'Christianity' – in the
flight of a bird of prey or in the tragedy of a shipwreck. This
allowed him to teach, better than in any church sermon (at
which he was notoriously hopeless), about the universality and
the omni-presence of Christ: Christ whom we 'know no longer
in an earthly way' but as a 'life-giving Spirit'.

The early church Fathers wrestled with the question of how
truth and holiness could have existed before the coming of
Christ. They found the answer in understanding what this
Coming or Incarnation really involved: the embodiment of the

Word. But the Word has always been, before the historical moment of the Incarnation, and it continues to be, both in time and beyond time. As the church itself now sees and teaches, the Word can operate outside of the faith that names and bows before the name of Jesus.

And as the prophets of our era have taught us, Merton, Rahner, Bede Griffiths, John Main among them, Christianity is at a crossroads at least as crucial to its future as when it left Jerusalem and journeyed to Rome. Now in the era which is seeing the formation of a new, global evolution of consciousness among humanity, Christians are being released from old limitations – from religious imperialism and intolerance – to see their Lord dance in a thousand places. We can only be humbled and elevated to be taught this by a human teacher like the Dalai Lama in whom the Word shines so strongly and whose life and teaching so clearly embody his message of peace, forgiveness and compassion.

Words which attempt to tell the truth are, of course, always risky. They can upset and mislead. But the experience of the Word requires we risk using them to communicate what can ultimately only be known in communion.

At the retreat we tried to articulate a vision of the future for our small but global Community of Christian meditation. We realised it was not a matter of predicting but of seeing the future, not the details but the essentials of what could be and what we wanted to be. Seeing the meaning of the present. Not fortune-telling but prophecy. It seemed to me that the future lies in the empowerment of more and more people to be voices, silent voices, of the Word we love and are absorbed by in the human and divine person of Jesus the risen Christ.

The Seminar helped to clarify our vision of the church's future just as, for many who spoke to me afterwards, it had deepened their faith in Christ. That future seems to invite the development of a contemplative Christianity, not concerned primarily with its numbers or institutional power. In such a church the spiritual formation we receive throughout our life, in home, community,

parish and school will not stop at words, will not defend propositions at the cost of charity, but will advance into the
experience of the Word itself.

A community of this kind will be one of growth, not of
embattled decline, and its self-communication will nourish the
earth. Its perception of God will teach it to be aware of the
ground of unity it enjoys with all peoples. Its discipleship of
Jesus will empower it to teach and celebrate his words in prayer,
liturgy and social action. Its receptivity to the Spirit will align it
with all the valid salvific movements of its day.

Such a vision should make us laugh with joy. Whenever old
fears and divisions are dissolved, transcendence ignites laughter. At the end of the Seminar the Dalai Lama told a joke to
illustrate a point. Retelling it in English, Thupten Jinpa, his
superb translator, lapsed (O, happy fault!) from his usual self-
control. Time and again as he tried to finish the joke he would
collapse in laughter and carried the entire hall with him. As
we rocked and wept with laughter nothing could have better
illustrated how deeply serious we were and what wonder and
joy the fresh hearing of the Word had been for us all.

With much love

Laurence

Laurence Freeman OSB

Letter Ten

December 1994

Dearest Friends,

This is the time of early morning frosts in England. The other day people got up to see an amazing world filled with frosted spider webs – on trees, over doors, on the wheels of cars. The intricate beauty of the webs and their profusion is usually unnoticed. Now their careful patterns were drawn clearly by the delicate frost and ice slivers clinging to their forms, seemingly too heavy for the webs to bear but swinging bravely in the cold wind. The Incarnation of the Word similarly allows us now to see what has always been present in creation and Jesus shows this to us with all the vulnerability of the human form. Making the unseen visible awakens our attention and so ignites the spirit of prayer and praise.

The transformation worked in human consciousness through the birth of Jesus is a 'showing' of who we truly are: St Leo the Great wrote, 'Learn, O Christian, how great is your dignity . . . you have been made a partaker in the divine nature.' This new way of seeing and knowing is what we celebrate in all the feasts of the church.

In London over the past few years, we have developed a tradition of holding a day of preparation for meditators just before the celebration of Christmas and Easter. On the Saturday before Christmas this year about 150 meditators, some from far afield, joined in the hall at the monastery of Christ the King at Cockfosters. Together we read and reflected on the story of the Nativity, meditated and celebrated the Eucharist in a spirit of silence and mindfulness.

It was the last major shopping day before Christmas. All around us there raged the frantic commercialism and entertainment industry which constitute the 'celebration' of Christmas in the post-Christian West. It was therefore all the more moving to be part of a small group of people who were trying to keep in touch with the deeper meaning of the festivities. By being together in word and silence we were learning the finer meaning of celebration, focusing attention on the Christ rather than on Santa Claus, and giving prime time to this end. Our celebration was fuelled by *lectio*, a quiet slow chewing of the word of scripture and by meditation, the silence beyond all words.

This letter reaches you after Christmas but still within the Christmas season, hopefully soon after Epiphany. In the light of the kind of celebration we enjoyed at our day at Cockfosters it is not too late to reflect on the meaning of this season. We can still ponder what has broken through the surface of reality and through the veil of confusion and ignorance which so often obscures reality for us. And ponder, too, on what it means to celebrate this kind of mystery.

Celebration is the way we integrate something of extraordinary importance into the ordinary round of our lives. The fun, food, and partying which accompany celebration are like ripples on life's surface caused by a deeper reality breaking through, of the unseen becoming visible. If there is only an artificial creation of surface disturbance, without the deeper, more silent reality emerging, celebration becomes hollow. Preparing for it becomes a cause of anxiety and the end result after all the fun is spent can be depression. For many people, celebrating Christmas without an awareness of Christ can lead to just this. The way we celebrate Christmastide defines the kind of person, as well as the kind of Christian, we are.

It is difficult, however, to celebrate any religious festival today. Paganism means the obstruction and obscuring of the sacredness of reality and the mistaking of images for reality. Modern paganism – we can call it consumerism – desacralises the sacred in ways that it is important for us to recognise. Firstly, it opposes the true spirit of celebration by encouraging excess – too much of everything. There is nothing puritanical about challenging a lack of moderation: too much food causes indigestion and indigestion prevents enjoyment! Celebration invites and requires moderation. The liberty of spirit that is needed for celebration grows out of such a freely embraced discipline. Christian scriptures frequently expose the pagan fallacy and give insight into the true way of celebrating life. They are passages, however, that have often become abused and misquoted and have become identified with life-denying repression.

For many people today even the word 'Christian' often spells constraint and denial rather than a path of wisdom showing the way to true en-joyment of life. Indeed in the face of materialism not many religious traditions do offer a strong alternative to the forces of consumerism which desacralise life by sentimentalising and trivialising reverence for the sacred. Behind the sentimentality of our now paganised religious festivals there can be found a dark rage against the sacred, a mockery of reverence in any form, an iconoclasm born of despair and cynicism. Yet any good, whole life requires a sustained awareness and appreciation of the sacred. Without a sense of the sacred, anxiety and depression readily flood our minds.

There are many forces that make true celebration difficult today. And, of course, many of these forces can be unconsciously interiorised and operate as inner resistances – the reluctance to take time to reflect on the meaning of what is celebrated, being too busy to meditate, or too demanding that meditation should produce instant and pleasurable results.

Re-learning the art of celebrating the sacred in life is a work for all religions today. Perhaps it can only be achieved if we somehow learn how to celebrate each other's religious feasts. This will be the fruit of true dialogue and meditation together, a sharing of the sacred symbols and insights proper to each tradition. Every religion has a mission to communicate the truth through its own symbols and traditions, not to compete with others. The founders of the great religions were not competitors. Neither should their followers try to force themselves into the place held by others at the banquet of the kingdom of heaven. Simply by communicating itself a religion fulfils its mission to awaken people to the sacred. Nothing more effectively disempowers the destructive forces of paganism than the true, unselfish joy of celebration among and between the followers of different religions.

Perhaps in time the different religions will learn to celebrate together. Meanwhile each must learn how to celebrate and communicate itself. For Christians, the liturgies of worship are both the way we celebrate and the way we communicate the truth of Christ. The tone of a liturgy reflects the health and depth of the church that is celebrating. It is itself the way the faith is shared. But merely adding noise and activity to what happens on the altar does not enhance a celebration. In order to celebrate the sacred we must at some moment, and at some level, be silent because the divinity we are celebrating lies beyond all expression. Liturgy is by nature an expression of faith and joy but it can only achieve this effectively if deep silence is woven into it. Meditation and liturgy need, therefore, to be re-integrated in Christian worship. Then the interior dimension of celebration and joy is awakened.

We will renew the celebration of the liturgy when we understand again that meditation is itself a celebration of life. To sit and meditate each day is no less a silent statement of faith in life, its source and meaning. Liturgy can best express this when it is inserted into the silence that is beyond expression.

Silence and celebration, then, are inextricably interwoven. We can wholeheartedly celebrate only what is full, what has in some way been completed, even if the point of plenitude that has been reached has not yet the final fullness of life. We celebrate a birthday because a year of life has been completed. We even celebrate a death as a birth into eternity because all the years of life have been completed.

Joy is the felt experience of fullness. It is joy, therefore, which is the energy of celebration. Joy is needed to celebrate; without it there is the feeling of forced fun or phoneyness. But joy is also enhanced and more fully released by genuine celebration. However, in contrast with the pleasures of consumerism, joy is unconditioned. It is wholly natural. It is our true nature to be joyful. It can rise in us wherever we are, whatever we may be feeling, whenever we are one with ourselves, not making any effort to be someone else. Joy is not bound to entertainment, to fun, distraction or even to the satisfaction of desire. We can be joyful in the midst of suffering.

In one of the greatest commentaries upon the birth of Jesus, St Leo the Great in the fifth century wrote that on this 'birthday of life . . . no one has the right to be sad'. His remark teaches us something of the nature of joy. It does not mean that we must pretend to be happy or feel guilty about suffering. It does, however, suggest an innate tendency of the ego to dip us toward sadness and into its many compound forms such as anger and depression. There are many points in the psyche where it is easier to submit to this tendency, to sink into sadness and isolation, rather than accept the upward wave of joy.

St Leo explains his affirmation of joy by saying that on this Day of Christ, the fear of death has been dispelled and the devil, the 'inventor of death', has been conquered. Because these are universal truths the cause of joy at the birth of Jesus is 'common to all'. The Christian can glimpse here a truth of great importance for modern Christianity. The universality of Christ is a unifying, not an excluding truth. The centrality of the Incarnation in terms of human history can only be measured by spiritual standards. It does not relegate other religions to the sidelines or denigrate the epiphanies of God that have occurred through them 'in many and varied ways'. Indeed the Epiphany of Christ gives higher definition to all the varied manifestations of God. Yet in Jesus an eye of consciousness has opened in the deepest ground of human nature.

Deep attention is required to realise this, attention both to the great symbols of revelation contained in scripture and to the ground of our own being. This attention is prayer and it is achieved through grace and the work of silence, day by day.

St Leo tells us that the 'singular birth' of Christ occurred in the 'fullness of time'. The fullness of time means the present moment: the opening of consciousness to reality which happens in meditation. Stillness of mind and silence bring about the descent of consciousness beneath the waves of thought and imagination, and the liberation of emotion from desire and sadness. However attached our minds may be to time, the faithfulness of meditation loosens those bonds. Faith sets us free, as St Leo says, to 'partake of the divine nature'. The bonds are always those of desire: either the affirmative desire that propels us impatiently forward through imagination to acquire something, or the reverse desire of sadness when we regret what we have lost or the opportunities we have missed. We have no right to be sad, no reason to fantasise, once we realise what has broken through the surface of time and shared its being with ours.

The fullness of time does not mean that clocks stop ticking. Life goes on. The time we allocate to meditate means a practical decision and rearrangement of daily priorities. But it does mean that during these times of meditation, however resilient may be the desires and regrets of our time-bound minds, human consciousness is gradually, imperceptibly, expanded beyond the restraints imposed by the mental concepts of past and future. We cannot know that we partake in the divine nature – and so cannot act as if we do – while we remain within those restraints. As freedom uncoils within the human person we are challenged to see life as a process of divinisation. The ultimate meaning of human experience is found in seeing it as the manifestation of God that shows through every human uniqueness.

In the mirror of human life, the birth and life of Jesus is the clearest revelatory image of this human meaning. 'God became Man so that Man might become God.' Life does not stop when this is understood and celebrated. The pagan ego, of course, fears that it will be extinguished. But rather than stopping, life is enhanced and energised. Life goes on in its ordinary way but it is lived and shared quite differently. As meditation dissolves the time-bound habits of desire, we are rendered more patient. And wisdom is the fruit of patience.

All of this is realised not through the attempt to achieve or master spiritual truths or reality, or by trying to win God's favour. It happens through the simple work of faith-filled attention. Nothing is more important for Christians today than to recover the sense of how faith and attention are related and how their integration is actually practised in meditation. Faith is more than the confession of dogma or orthodox adherence to a group of believers. Attention is more than thinking about the dogma or the symbols of what we believe.

Meditation, as John Main said, verifies the truths of faith in our own experience. This happens because attention deepens and purifies our consciousness. As this act of attention is a movement of love from the depth of human nature there is no point where we stop paying attention. Do we ever say 'I have loved you enough' to someone we love? The unlimited nature of love means that we must inevitably, at some point, discover the sacrificial nature of love as the total offering up of the gift of self-consciousness.

The work of all attention, such as the work of the mantra itself, is like passing through a deep, long tunnel. There are times when the tunnel bends and the light at the other end is no longer there to encourage us. There are times, too, when the sides of the tunnel – the discipline of attention – seem constricting and narrow. At many points of the journey it is tempting to stop or go back.

In the fullness of time, however, the work of attention is realised: not when we attain what we are attending to but when we altogether lose our grip on the sense of ourselves paying attention. Attention can never be complete while we are self-conscious. This is why in the work of the mantra we are not finished just because the mind has temporarily found calmness or peace or even when thought seems to have been stilled. It is not truly stilled until we have stopped thinking of ourselves. ('The monk who thinks that he is praying is not truly praying.') The work of the mantra takes on a new refinement and gentleness of love at those points when it is most tempting to give it up.

Every tunnel has an end, which is also a new opening. At that point in the work of meditation the little 'I' of the ego is sacrificed through the greater love of the Self and dissolves in the light of Christ which is itself the God who is light. Then what we felt as the walls of the tunnel dissolve and are seen to be no more than the imagination of the ego.

This has all already happened in human nature through the Incarnation in the fullness of time. But it has to penetrate through all the successive layers of consciousness through the combined work of divine grace and human faith. We call this human existence. As soon as this work is consciously attended to, by the commitment we make to a spiritual path, we begin to become aware of different levels of reality. This enhanced awareness is the end of religious fundamentalism, which is essentially limited to the mental and egoic levels of consciousness. It is also the beginning of a new way of living life, day by day, as a celebration of the gift of being, with thankfulness and joy at the deep centre of our being.

Until this spiritual sense is awakened and we become aware of the deeper levels of consciousness, life is perceived exclusively in terms of mental perception. The mind is like a pane of glass. We can see through it at times, though always with the feeling of separateness, of something between us and what we see. At other times the transparency of the mind becomes opaque and it merely mirrors back to us our own cloudy thoughts and feelings. Clarity or translucency of mind is of course preferable to the state of muddied self-centredness. But the invitation of Christian spirituality is to more than mental calm and clarity. It is to be re-born, trans-figured and re-newed through the mind of Christ as a fully conscious part of his Body.

We accept that invitation not only by moral goodness but by the work of deep attention, pure prayer. As an early Christian monk once wrote, 'The effects of keeping the commandments do not suffice to heal the powers of the soul completely. They must be complemented by a contemplative activity . . . and this activity must penetrate the spirit' (Evagrius, *Praktikos* 79).

It is not only the act of attention but what our attention unites us to, which brings about our complete healing and salvation. Because of the transformation of human nature that occurred in the Incarnation it is only necessary for us to pay full, undivided attention to our own nature, to be silently, unstrivingly natural, for this transformation of consciousness, or awakening, to happen.

It is what we see through the pane of consciousness in the particular moments of the Nativity, the Baptism of Christ and the marriage feast at Cana: the collective feast of Epiphany. These are historical moments in the life of Jesus of Nazareth, separated from us by time and space. Yet their deepest significance flows from the fullness of time, the present moment, which they express and toward which they point those who are celebrating the feast. In that dimension of consciousness these signs, like all that Jesus said and did, become powerful symbols – or sacraments – of divinity.

Every meditator knows that one of the consequences of the practice of pure prayer is the deepening of consciousness, the awareness that there are levels of reality corresponding to the deeper layers of consciousness. The deepening of faith does not mean the reinforcement of mental consciousness – making dogma more definite or inflexible. The Letter to the Hebrews warns against this when it urges us, 'Let us then stop discussing the rudiments of Christianity . . . instead, let us advance towards maturity' (Hebrews 6:1–2). To deepen faith means to deepen consciousness, to deepen prayer.

Deeper silence and stillness in prayer allows grace to do its work in us and to manifest the reality that Christ embodies in his mystical Body. At the mental level, through the pane of the mirror-mind, reality is seen dualistically and we therefore relate to it in ways that frequently, inevitably, lead to conflict. As we journey deeper, this double vision gradually resolves, simplifies and unifies, and conflict resolves into peace. Meditation affects these conflicts within ourselves, in our families and communities, within society and between nations, because all conflict takes root in this fundamental division in consciousness itself.

God, 'imagined' in the mind, is then realised in the heart. And, in the simultaneous knowledge that arises both of God and of the true Self, God is embraced as self-communicating love. The paradigm of this meeting of God with humanity is the birth in Bethlehem.

Whenever someone fully communicates him or her self to another person, human consciousness is confronted with the unknown and the boundless. The pane of the mind is dissolved. In human relationships this is an exceptionally rare occurrence. The glass often seems tragically unbreakable even in the emergencies of life. But it is possible to penetrate it and it is the natural fruit of faithful love, perhaps nurtured through many difficult years. Although not always dramatic, self-communication is by nature sacrificial. This does not mean self-destructive, though something of us, of course, does not survive a true gift of self.

Self-giving is an invitation to self-transcendence. When we encounter a true gift of self in another we are faced with an unavoidable challenge to respond in kind. The gift of self must be unconditional. Its invitation to respond must be infinitely patient and uncoercive. It is, therefore, the heart of *ahimsa*, nonviolence. The Beatitudes of Jesus are the enlightened facets of this jewel of human self-giving.

Incarnation and Resurrection are the supreme sacraments of the unity of self-giving and self-transcendence. As sacraments they work on us by the power of their own reality but they also invite and impel a response from anyone who welcomes them into their life. The archetypal truth of self-giving is manifested from within the deepest core of divinity in the birth of Jesus. In contemplating the Christmas story, preferably perhaps after the

Christmas sales in the quiet infancy of the new year and in the rich symbolism of the Epiphany, a deeper sense and understanding of God emerges.

Rather than the God of power and might, Lord and Jehovah, true celebration helps us to see through this mirror-image of our own fantasies of what 'it would be like to be God'. We see the true nature of God as Love. All-powerful because all-loving, all-loving because wholly self-giving. The silent symbol of the child of Bethlehem preaches the deepest wisdom of human and divine vulnerability and the strange, disturbing truth that our ultimate security and peace is to be found in the risk of self-giving.

It is so important for a true celebration of Christmas to release the power of these symbols and truths. The sentimentality of Christmas, replacing Jesus by a department store Santa, is in the strictest sense a sacrilege. The churches are challenged to rediscover the true spirit of celebration and worship by contemplating the Christmas stories so deeply and joyfully that they must inevitably be led to rest in stillness and silence. Just as individuals are changed by deep attention, by pure prayer, so will all the communities of Christianity. From self-protection and caution we move to self-giving and love.

The great Christian truths can only effectively be communicated in the self-giving of Christian life. These are truths about God, human beings and love. They tell us that God is infinite and transcendent, personal love; that human beings embody the paradox of a free destiny to share in the divine nature; and that the meaning and purpose of life is to realise the unity of human and divine love. But these truths remain inspiring abstractions until they are embodied. The 'singular birth' of Jesus – in the eternal womb of the Father, in Bethlehem, in our own individual hearts – embodies them. It brings the truth home to us.

Meditation is, for all these reasons, a most Christian way of prayer and true worship. Far from being a mind-game or a form of 'mental prayer', meditation is the incarnation of prayer. In stillness, body and mind are integrated in the non-duality of the spirit. It is not then we who are praying but we who become prayer, fully conscious and fully alive.

Any newborn child belongs most intimately to its family, but also to the world. It is also a new arrival to the human race who share a collective love and responsibility for it. This is something recognised both by law and by sentiment. The child of Bethlehem very clearly belongs to humanity as a whole, not only to the Jewish or Christian families. Every epiphany of his true self through his life and teaching manifests his universality. Every child, from the moment of its birth, even of its conception, also transforms the family it is born into. Unconsciously it effects a revolution in the life-style and relationships that constitute the family. Very clearly, too, Jesus has changed the world. To see why and how he continues to do so, we must look not so much at the mirror of history as into the depth of our own heart.

St Leo once preached that the 'birthday of the Lord is the birthday of peace' and that 'peace it is that gives birth to the children of God'. May the pilgrimage of meditation engender this peace in our life this year, as individuals and as a community, and empower us all to share it generously with others.

With much love

Laurence

Laurence Freeman OSB

Letter Eleven

March 1995

Dearest Friends,

Once upon a time a famous saint was thirsty. He sent his disciple off to get him a glass of water. But while he was getting the water, the saint, who had a slight tendency to that kind of thing, became rapt in an ecstasy. The disciple returned with the water to find his master beyond human reach and so he sat and waited patiently, the glass of water in his hand. The ecstasy lasted for many days. When finally the saint returned to normal consciousness his first thought and first words were to ask for the glass of water.

Versions of this story are told in many contemplative traditions, not to exalt the state of ecstasy, but to show how it is not the true test of spiritual perfection. Ecstasies may come and go and they do not necessarily make us better human beings. St Paul wrote (2 Corinthians 12) about his visions and revelations and of the ecstasy in which he had been lifted up to the 'third heaven'. But what he boasted of, he said, were his weaknesses. He came to know the true power of God through these, his mysterious 'thorn in the flesh', and not his spiritual ecstasies.

This is so obvious and central a Christian idea that it is usually forgotten. It is not, of course, exclusively Christian, but of all religions Christianity is the most emphatically based on the paradox of strength and weakness, death and resurrection. The total powerlessness of the cross erects a principle of self-criticism and humility in the heart of Christianity before which all spiritual or institutional might must ultimately bow. So whenever Christians exalt mystical experiences as proof of holiness or institutional strength as a sign of spiritual truth they deviate from the example of Christ who did not make miracles the basis of faith and who rejected terrestrial power.

Yet as history and daily experience show, Christians can easily and willingly slip into superstition and the worship of power. As Jesus' disciples showed as they walked with him, human nature has a powerful tendency to superstition and authoritarianism. So it is not surprising that we are still learning how to follow our teacher as much through our failures as through our obedience.

We can so quickly drift from the truth which has once touched, inspired or even transfigured us. Yet it is not individual experiences but patterns of behaviour embedded in habit and style of life which are the real test of our nature and the direction we are going. When Cassian wrote about human failures in compassion or purity of heart, he warned us not to judge ourselves negatively on the basis of our individual lapses, but to look more wisely at the underlying patterns and drives in our character. Doing this, we avoid the trap of reinforcing guilt reactions and we come instead to true insight, self-knowledge and so to the humility which effects real change. Better to know oneself, said an early monk, than to work miracles.

Think again of the story of the thirsty saint and of what it means. Does it mean only that after ecstasy we return to the needs of daily life? I think it points to something deeper than the duality between flesh and spirit – to the nature of the mind as every meditator experiences it day by day.

From time to time, by grace and faith and the simplicity of the mantra, we can be led into deep peace and equanimity. Our conscious existence becomes harmonious, reflecting from deep in our being the calm and joy of Christ's risen life. Body and mind and spirit are married in peace, like a couple who after much arguing return to the basic goodness and love of their relationship. As far as it is concerned, the mind sees its interminable internal monologues and self-dramatising anxieties suddenly drop away, wonderfully calmed. It becomes silent, amazed at its own capacity to be still (perhaps not aware that by thinking it is not yet wholly still!) and at its capacity to let go of its compulsive desires and fears.

These experiences are not ecstatic because we are still very conscious of what we are feeling. But they are nonetheless good feelings and they nourish us in ways that fill us with gratitude and spontaneous praise. They help us understand the scriptural injunction to 'praise the Lord'. For a while we are able to praise, empowered to fulfil the spirit of the injunction, not merely to write the Lord a polite letter of thanks.

Then there are times – perhaps fleeting moments – when we are led entirely out of ourselves. We are not asleep. But neither are we awake in the usual sense. Indeed, compared with this, our usual waking state is more like a dream than waking. The clarity of consciousness we enjoy is because the I who wants to enjoy it has disappeared.

'I live no longer but Christ lives in me.' Is St Paul who describes this trans-personal, ego-transcendent state a Buddhist or a pantheist? Who was the I who lived no longer? Who is the me in whom only Christ, the perfect image of the invisible God, lives? These are important, endless questions. But their importance only takes effect after the event. In the duration of the simple state of union these questions, like all thoughts, are consumed by the sheer presence of the 'One who truly is'.

For us, as for the thirsty saint, these experiences of spiritual consolation or of ecstasy are mortal. We return to ordinary reality and remember the last thought we had before the experience happened – our thirst, our bank overdraft, the troubles our children are facing. Before long we are engrossed in our familiar thought-worlds. God becomes a goal we are trying to achieve or understand, or a memory we feel nostalgic for, rather than the I AM of love who floods our inmost being.

The early Christian monks well understood these passing states of the spiritual life. Cassian wrote of the 'lethal sleep' of

prayer when the mind enjoys a lulled activity and dulled feelings. It is a form of the 'Gethsemani sleep' of the apostles.
Cassian also described the 'pernicious peace', a strong phrase
referring to the emotional and mental calm we try to cling to
as soon as we become aware of it. None of these states, of
ecstasy, sleep or consolation, are the goal of prayer. However
attractive they may be, or painful their loss, there is another
goal. A condition of complete simplicity requiring not less than
everything, as Dame Julian put it. Poverty of spirit, purity of
heart. The combined state of the Beatitudes. Life in Christ.

In terms which all traditions can use it is the state where the
mind is merged with the heart, not just for a few timeless
moments but permanently and unwaveringly. Like a candle
burning in a windless space. Like the man who built his house
on the rock of the true Self rather than on the sands of the ego.

Our daily experience in meditation proves all this. So does
our collective experience as the church. Every week churches
are filled (at least some are) with clergy and laity reading the
scriptures, celebrating the mystery of Christ's presence in
Eucharist and fellowship, and exchanging the sign of peace. We
celebrate the teaching of Jesus as the master of compassion,
forgiveness and wisdom. We pledge ourselves in all sincerity to
follow. These are precious and necessary times in our weekly,
daily lives. But we can easily be lulled by the religious atmosphere of it all, by the weekly routines we don't like changed, by
the reassuring calm of obedient laity sitting still in their pews
instructed by the qualified clergy.

How well do our parishes and communities and institutional
Christianity live what they hear preached? Why do we seem so
riven with feuds, disputes, power struggles, plotting for suc-
cession, and mutual excommunications? Or, has it ever been so
different? Were not the seeds of all this evident in the apostles'
jockeying for power next to Jesus? Were not most of St Paul's
words addressed to Christians in conflict with each other? Look
at the Reformation, at European history . . .

It is not a question of anyone's sincerity being called into doubt. Religious people, especially those in robes, as Jesus remarked, can be terrifyingly and ruthlessly sincere. Sincerity without love is the problem. It is the demise of tolerance, compassion and the forgiveness of enemies in the conduct of their religious duties which condemns Christians.

Facing the modern crisis of Christianity means we should accept everyone's sincerity. Our concern, however, should not be only for the political outcome of these many conflicts of sincerity which are tearing the church apart. It is not about whether progressives or conservatives win out – whatever those terms mean anyway. Was Jesus who obeyed the Law faithfully and yet denounced false religion a conservative or a radical? Politically, the pendulum swings continuously. It is up to good people to try to ensure that it doesn't sweep away too many innocent victims as it swings.

More important than ecclesiastical politics is how the present state of Christianity affects the way Christians are able to fulfil their mission. Their faith itself is a mission. Jesus tells us to go out, beyond ourselves and our familiar, safe worlds, to heal and to proclaim that the kingdom of God is at hand (Matthew 10:7). In the past, Christians have often believed that theirs was the only religion with the right of mission. They frequently ridiculed or persecuted other faiths. But in doing that Christians both betrayed and demeaned their faith. Their intolerance prevented them from seeing in what their own extraordinary and amazing uniqueness really consisted. Whenever religions fail to reverence what is unique in each other they fall, like all other competing groups, into the ego's drives of desire and fear and anger.

One of my own deepest concerns has become the terrible failure of Christianity to communicate its unique message.

In the western world, the historical heartland of Christianity, the authority and credibility of the church has been devastated. At least a second generation are reaching maturity deprived of the spiritual teaching and training they should have received from within their own culture and tradition. Yet the churches continue their internal strife with unevangelical bitterness, while claiming to 'evangelise' the post-Christian world. If we cannot find unity and love deeper than our differences of opinion, can we even take ourselves seriously, let alone expect others to?

I said to the Dalai Lama last September that I thought Christians should be grateful for his visits to the West because he restored a good name to religion. I also meant that by entering such deep and open dialogue with us he was mysteriously helping us see more clearly the uniqueness of our own faith. If Christian leaders could similarly risk themselves in dialogue with other faiths they might find that the level of internal division within their churches would diminish. If they could listen to the questions which the unchurched and the churchless would like to put to them they might find their mission was better fulfilled.

Let us consider for the rest of this letter some of these questions from those outside the church who wonder who or what we are.

For so many outside the church, Christianity is just that, a *church*. It seems a religious institution whereas Buddhism, Hinduism or Sufism seem to be more spiritual, more concerned with personal, inner transformation. It is not a flattering comparison for Christianity to be identified with policing moral behaviour and controlling belief rather than with deepening spiritual growth. But it cannot be lightly dismissed.

Of course, no religion is without its 'institutional' structures and their attendant faults. All Asian religions, too, have their factions, feuds and farces. Where western moral values have impacted on society the religious leaders are increasingly urging moral reform. In Buddhism the principle of 'right belief' is the cause of as much theologising as in Christianity – and of as many different views. What has led Christianity, however, to such an excessive emphasis on institutional control and protection of orthodoxy is almost an accident of history – which history is correcting.

The primitive church saw itself as a body of followers of the

'Way' and their life had a dynamic sense of pilgrimage. The destination was, as St Augustine said, simply the 'vision of God'. In the days of persecution religion was in every sense what it should always be, a matter of life and death. But once Christianity had become the official state religion its numbers grew so fast that, as St Ambrose said, the church was like St Peter's boat, so full of fish it was in danger of sinking. Religious observance became more formalistic. Orthodoxy became confused with the battle-lines of political power and identified with the virtues of respectability and obedience rather than with the mind's ecstatic insight into the nature of truth.

So what is different here between Christianity and the 'spiritual' religions of Asia is not the goal of spiritual development but the history of the religion. Christianity's hierarchical imagery, descending from the revelation of the divine Creator, was used to reinforce both ecclesiastical and secular power-structures, often in stark disobedience to Christ's call to a ministry of humble service. Later, this imagery of hierarchy was applied to the idea of racial and religious superiority in the centuries of western imperialism.

It would be foolish and false to reduce 1,600 years of 'institutional Christianity' to this. It is less than half the picture. But it would be hard-hearted of Christians not to see the errors of history, to repent of them, and to root out the vestiges of those historical patterns still influencing their current thinking and practice. By doing this we can better understand how the present disintegration of Christianity as a state religion has brought about such self-destructive polarisations.

Yet in this massive death there are brilliant seeds of rebirth. Freed from identifying religion with respectability, faith with blind obedience and orthodoxy with uniformity, Christians can again remember what they are about, what they are for.

Early Christians lived out the search for the vision of God in a pure heart through poverty of spirit. This goal is both unique to Christianity and its common ground with other faiths. To see God in the Christian sense means to experience at every level of our humanity, including the physical and mental, a union in love with the Trinity of love through the total humanity of Jesus, the incarnation of the second person of that Trinity.

Yet any human being striving for poverty of spirit can easily recognise his or her own experience of faith and failure, hope and despair, in the lives of seekers of other faiths. Similarly, any humble Christian can recognise the achievement of purity of heart in any individual, whether Mahatma Gandhi or Mother Teresa. Meditating with people of different faiths proves all this in experience very quickly. We see how silence is the quickest cure for intolerance and the best antidote for religious arrogance.

For many Christians, however, these are new and bewildering ideas. Leadership is needed to avoid rashly labelling these ideas as heretical merely because they are strange. Leadership is required to make these ideas familiar and to show how deeply true to the tradition of Christ they are.

The old imperial arrogance of the church claiming to be the sole repository of truth and the sole guardian of the ways of holiness has been officially disowned. But the ways of thinking it engendered prevail in many quarters. Of course, these 'new' ideas are as old as the church. The questions they raise about the uniqueness of Christianity and its mission are our modern challenge. But they are forms of questions which all religions must face today as they also try to redefine themselves in relation to modern consciousness. Buddhists, for example, must face their tendency to see theism as a 'lower' level of spiritual development, just as Christians must confront their often ill-informed rejection of Buddhism as atheistic and self-centred.

The Roman Catholic Church has tackled this problem with great courage and honesty since the Second Vatican Council. Against all the odds, a major religious institution, one heavily self-insulated against the world around it, sat down in front of the world and criticised itself. This work of the Holy Spirit goes on still in Christianity – with leaps forward as well as tragic setbacks. With such a complex history and so rich a diversity of communities and theologies it must be a long haul.

During the Council, Christians were able to face their historical failures over tolerance, against Jews and other faiths. In so doing they were empowered to state a number of forgotten truths about the uniqueness of Christianity. They did this, significantly, by affirming the goodness and holiness of other faiths, not merely proclaiming their own. The Council showed a basic Christian truth that through repentance and honest self-knowledge comes the truth that sets us free.

The Christian Fathers of the second and third centuries had the same struggle in the terms of their age. If Jesus was the Son of God, how did he relate to the truth in Jewish or Greek traditions? Today we must extend this question to embrace eastern religions, and the tool for doing so is the same as for the early Fathers: the theology of the Logos. For the Greeks the Logos expressed the inherent reasonableness and order in the cosmos. The eternal Logos, according to St John, became flesh in a particular human being in a way both unparalleled and unrepeatable. But these terms do not demean other traditions. The generous cosmic theology of the Logos and the Incarnation work by affirming and illuminating rather than by defeating or subordinating. When his disciples tried to stop a man not of their group from performing miracles Jesus rebuked them: 'Do not stop him, for he who is not against you is on your side' (Luke 9:50).

Many westerners today who have received no transmission of Christian faith look at Christianity with renewed interest when they see Christians meditating. The very phrase 'Christian meditation' excites their curiosity. They see Christians recovering a new depth of spiritual experience, a faith more integrated with style of life, a stronger personal knowledge of Jesus and a more self-confident relationship to other faiths.

Meditation does not seek to infiltrate or pilfer from other traditions. But it does open to anyone the possibility of entering the Christian path by mature choice at a serious spiritual depth. By their commitment to the daily discipline of meditation Christians help show how directly related it is, as a way of prayer, to the core of the human mystery. Much more than a technique of self-improvement, it is a way of self-transcendence. More than a way of relaxation, it is a way into the peace beyond all understanding. More than method or technique, it institutes at the heart of your life an orientation, an attitude, an inner transformation, a way of living. As an early Christian teacher once wrote, the way we pray is the way we believe.

The essentials of meditation are deeply complementary between different paths. When meditators sit and discuss the difficulties and the fruits of meditation they discover they are often talking of the same experience in different words. At the same time the differences are important, because it matters greatly that you meditate within a particular tradition. It would be difficult to imagine a serious meditator without a tradition. As the Dalai Lama says on *The Good Heart* video, just sitting down and closing your eyes is not meditation. Serious practice usually identifies the tradition you most essentially belong to.

With the teaching of John Main and others, many Christians have been able to meditate with a confident sense of support from the tradition of their own faith. They no longer have to leave it in order to find guidance or community. Of course, for many Christians meditation can still seem something eastern and suspicious or syncretistic. Part of the work of our Community is supportive to those already meditating. But an important part, too, is educational, reminding Christians that their own contemplative tradition does have an apophatic or deeply silent prayer.

Wherever fear reigns, you find it originates in ignorance and expresses itself in violence. This is evident in most forms of religious fundamentalism. Not everything conservative is fundamentalist, of course, but neither is conservatism always well-educated. A simple positive step to overcome ignorance and expand openness would be to encourage the Christian reading of other scriptures. The love of the biblical Word could only be deepened by this grassroots dialogue.

Young western Buddhists are often as unaware as Christians

that there is a rich contemplative literature in Christianity. Our prayer books have been pious but sadly lacking in representation from the church Fathers, the Desert tradition, the Cistercian fathers, the English or Spanish mystical schools. Usually this was because pastors felt this was beyond the simple minds of their flock.

What Christianity does not have is the more analytical and precise investigative studies of the process of transformation which you find, for example, in Buddhism. Psychology in the western Christian tradition, which was practised by the Desert Fathers, became alienated from religion with Freud. The exploration of the mechanisms of conversion and enlightenment can be greatly assisted by psychology provided it is operating from the right centre and with an adequate picture of the whole person. Until recently psychology had become almost wholly ego-centred. But with the revival of the Christian contemplative tradition and with the influence of eastern thought a much needed reintegration of psychology and spirituality is taking place. This would open up a whole new meaning for theology as knowledge of God.

For modern westerners God can be a big problem, or more specifically the prevalent image of God can be. The idea that God is inaccessible to humans except when we are punished by 'him' operates strongly in the minds of many who have rejected or bypassed Christianity. They are fascinated to hear Christians speaking of the knowledge or vision of God as something transformative and within our reach.

It makes sense to them that we can only know God to the degree we know ourselves. As I cannot know myself very well unless I know you, the commandment of loving both one's friends and one's enemies begins to make sense. In the past, Christian moral teaching rather inverted the order of reality by stressing the priority of loving God even before one had learned what it meant to love oneself. First love yourself is the law of nature on which grace then operates. There is no quicker way to do that than to meditate. You thereby quickly find out how

much you don't love yourself, how much conflict, self-rejection
or self-hatred you must face and dispel. By risking to love ourselves we discover that we cannot love God as an object but
only by sharing in God's own agape or creative Self-love. This
in turn begins to make sense of the Holy Spirit whom Jesus
released to lead us into the divine life.

A simple sign that we are growing in the vision of God is that
we are able to recognise images of God as images and give up
worshipping them as idols. An even more tangible sign is that
in situations where you formerly felt fear or denial you are now
able to see meaning and purpose. In what you once thought
ugly you now find beauty. The smelly tramp huddled in the shop
doorway becomes an epiphany of God.

For many people who see no spiritual depth in Christianity,
our good works and charities seem admirable. But they often
feel that they do not connect with an overall philosophy of
compassion. We speak so much of love but we are rarely seen
to be loving each other. Christians, however, do have a philosophy of compassion as deep and rich as that of any tradition,
despite our frequent failings in showing it to each other in our
institutions. Prayer is the foundation of compassion. And we
learn to pray in the school or workshop of community and
human relationships. You cannot live in community without
being hurled into self-knowledge and we need skills to persevere in that. There is a wise chapter on the 'Tools of Good
Works' in the Rule of St Benedict which reminds one of the
Buddhist's 'skilful means'. With advice like 'never let the sun go
down on your anger' or 'never give a false peace', Benedict
shows how compassion is learned by practice, and how universally recognisable are its wisdom and its fruits.

A Buddhist asked me recently, 'How can the Church now
communicate its new spiritual deepening and inspire people to
rediscover their faith?' It's a good question, from a good source.

There are a number of levels to the answer. Firstly, perhaps,
Christianity can re-present itself through brave, ongoing institutional reform. This does not mean seeking to be politically

correct on all issues. It does mean taking account of fundamental changes in modern consciousness with regard, for example, to the role of women and to basic human rights of freedom of speech and representation in the community one helps to support.

Secondly, Christian leaders need to exemplify honesty and openness in their way of leading. Then they can help shift the emphasis in Christianity to the inner life of spiritual development. This would mean that we might see the great potential of the parish realised: a local community oriented to the spiritual development of each individual while retaining the unity of diverse personalities.

Along with prophetic leadership, I think the most important aspect of Christianity's renewal is the small group. We have always been a faith embodied in small cells. Our own Community's contribution to the life of the church is particularly expressed in the small meditation groups which meet quietly together each week to be, to be more fully and deeply in the presence of the Lord and to be more deeply united with each other and in him.

If in small groups like this, Christian life can come alive, then the mind of Christ is realised in this age. The church as his mystical body will be transformed and perfected as a sign of his universal love and compassion. And each individual within those cells will be brought fully alive within and beyond their individuality. Despite their frequent lapses and many faults they will not be able to stop themselves from communicating the peace and joy of Christ in us.

With much love

Laurence

Laurence Freeman OSB

Letter Twelve

June 1995

Dearest Friends,

From the Corcovada, one of the highest points in Rio de Janeiro, 700 metres up, an immense statue of Christ extends its arms over and towards the whole city. Its standing shape makes it a cross. But the sign of suffering and death is metamorphosed into an embrace of unconditional love gathering in saints and sinners, aristocrats and drug dealers, the urchin children foraging on the streets and the well-mannered children wearing private school uniforms. The Corcovada Christ is a thrilling symbol of constancy in compassion and its bright white form catches your eye at nearly every turn as you travel around the city. It is movingly still, an ever-active, ever watchful presence.

There is a beautiful view from Corcovada, of course. Most cities can look beautiful from above, just as the world looks deceptively simple from a plane. But when you descend to the streets another picture develops over the tourist board's image. In Rio it is hard to reconcile the poverty and anarchy of the favellas, the inner city slum-villages, with the beauty and elegance of a city upon which these have developed as new hybrid forms of human living.

The Christ of Corcovada is an icon of the new understanding of God which Jesus spoke his word of life to communicate, and which he embodies. It can symbolise for the people of Rio and for us a new relationship with God and so with each other which the Spirit of Jesus is still trying to communicate to the world through the church. It tells us that we no longer need to play mental games with a god who rewards the virtuous and punishes the wicked. As long as those arms remain outstretched they remind us of the 'heavenly Father, who makes his sun rise on good and bad alike, and sends the rain on the honest and dishonest' (Matthew 5:45–6). Being in relationship with such a God alters forever the way we experience sin and grace and therefore life as a compound of sin and grace.

The Christian understanding of God helps us see sin not only in the crimes that make the favellas places of fear and cruelty but also in all the respectable structures of law-abiding society that make the favellas necessary. When injustice, cruelty and callousness encounter the unconditional love of God which empowers us to practise in his image, then sin dissolves. It is exposed as no more than the distance between us and reality, the illusion of separateness and self-sufficiency. Union and interdependence are realised and grace appears, not as a reward, but as the ever-present force of the divine compassion.

We share an awful responsibility for the consequences of sin in the world yet the Word of Christ does not allow us to remain focused on the world of sin. In the Christian vision sin is no longer an impediment to our entering the kingdom of God, the direct and personal union with God in the here and now. The kingdom, as John Main said, is not a place we are going to but rather an experience we carry within us on every breath. Indeed the constancy of the outstretched arms transforms sin as impediment into sin as opportunity. The Christian can sing of the *felix culpa*, the 'happy fault' of Adam, and Julian of Norwich can even say that 'sin is behovely'. 'Where sin was thus multiplied, grace immeasurably exceeded it' (Romans 5:20).

If the power of love can so reverse our usual sense of order – and love is always doing that – it can also teach us that God does not punish sin. As the great theologians have taught, sin contains its own punishment and, as psychology has made us realise, we are the most efficient punishers of ourselves. The distance between illusion and reality, a literally imaginative distance, is the measurement of hell.

A simple contemplation of the great symbols of Christ's love – the Eucharist, the cross, marriage, new life and a second chance – helps to shift awareness from sin to joy. The terrible curse of sin is joylessness. Sin-centred, moralistic religion is inevitably joyless and consequently hostile or suspicious towards joy. It thinks that joy is a sign of irreverence or a lack of seriousness. If joy were only the pleasure derived from satisfying appetites and ambitions then this would be true. But as I was reminded, by the joy and affectionate warmth I found among the Brazilians, especially the poor whom I had the pleasure of meeting, the joy of being does not depend upon satisfaction but upon celebration.

A social worker in one of the favellas told me how many rich young people came there to party, to dance (and, of course, to buy drugs). An American sister in Recife who has lived in a favela for fifteen years invited me to visit her joyful community of three living alongside their poor, but smiling neighbours. A Franciscan priest, living very poorly in Olinda, has taught meditation for some years already to his visitors and groups since he read John Main's *Word into Silence*. The small monastery of Goias which has turned itself decisively towards the poor with whom they celebrate and meditate each day has a lot to teach larger institutions about the joy which St Benedict says should characterise the monastic life. Like love, joy confounds all our mental arrangements of reality, changes the patterns of our expectations and assumptions. It comes when and how we cannot predict, like the Son of Man who comes when we least expect him (Matthew 24:44).

The polar opposites of life, like the problem of poverty and wealth or the relationship in the spiritual life between contemplation and action, can torment us individually and divide us socially. In Brazil I was constantly challenged to look deeper into the relevance of meditation to society. The challenge, and the wonderful people with whom I was meditating, helped me to see poverty of spirit (our non-possessiveness) as the crucial link between ourselves and those who lack the necessary possessions for human life. Meditation may not change the unjust social structures directly but through poverty of spirit it relentlessly dissolves the egotistical mental structures of fear and desire which create and sustain those institutions. It allows the middle class to look steadily at the poor without the fear of being robbed or the guilt of being accused; and so to see them in a way that includes rather than rejects or evades.

The contemplation of the great symbols of Christ's love develops our own attitudes in a more Christlike way. Towards sin, for example we become less self-rejecting and thus less judgemental of others. This kind of contemplation too helps to explain why the important liberation theologians of Latin America who have contributed so much to the life of the church have become recently more explicitly concerned with the contemplative dimension of faith. The marriage of contemplation and action is of course a matter of daily experience for the meditator. The way in which the daily practice illuminates these social and ecclesial questions also highlights the commitment to meditation itself, as a journey of faith. Like all journeys it takes us into itself step by step. Understanding this in terms of our ordinary experience dispels some of the mist from meditation which makes some observers see schism where there is in fact only a deepening power of unity.

A little diagram can help to show the levels of consciousness we all touch and pass through on the pilgrimage of meditation. Like all diagrams, and like the psycho-mystical systems of the great teachers of the tradition, it can also confuse if we think that it says everything or if we try to force our own experience to conform totally to it. Like a map it is meant to be used by anyone and so it is based on universal experience, but each one of us makes a unique journey and our own personal experience interprets the map even as we follow it. Meditation is a work, both our work of seeking God and God's work of seeking us. It is also a pilgrimage through the mysterious universe of the human person, an exploration into self-knowledge where the transcendence of egoism allows the unitive, non-dual knowledge of God to emerge. The meaning and the authenticity of our life depend upon this self-knowledge.

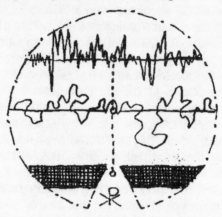

First level

Anyone who has ever sat down to be still immediately engages the first level of consciousness a little below the immediate surface of the mind's daily functioning awareness. It is a rude awakening to the degree of indiscipline and restlessness in our monkey minds. St Teresa compared it to a ship whose crew has mutinied, tied up the captain and is chaotically taking it in turns to steer the ship. Some days may be better than others in terms of distractedness but even that only proves how wayward our surface mind is, how dependent on external conditions, how uncentred we are. So, we sit down, we start to say the mantra with faith and attention. Within three seconds (on a good day) we are drawing up a shopping list, or deciding what to wear in the evening or rehearsing the phone call we forgot to make earlier.

'Therefore I bid you put away anxious thoughts about food and drink to keep you alive, and clothes to cover your body. Surely life is more than food, the body more than clothes' (Matthew 6:25). We aim to be still in the present moment which is the only moment of reality, of encounter with the God who is 'I Am'. Yet within seconds we are thinking thoughts of yesterday, making plans for tomorrow or weaving daydreams and wish-fulfilment in the realm of fantasy. 'Set your mind on God's kingdom and his justice before everything else, and all the rest will come to you as well. So do not be anxious about tomorrow; tomorrow will look after itself' (Matthew 6:33). Jesus' teaching on prayer is simple and pure, incisively wise and common-sensical. Yet it seems way beyond our capacity to practise it. Was he really speaking to ordinary humanity at all?

The discovery of our surface distractions is humbling. So, it helps to remember that it is a universal discovery – why else did Cassian recommend the mantra (he called it a 'formula') – sixteen hundred years ago? Yet our own age has added to the problem of natural distraction by the enormous mass of information and stimulus which we must swim through every day, trying to absorb and classify it all from the moment we turn on the radio in the morning to when we turn off the television at night.

At this discovery it is easy to be discouraged and to turn away from meditation. 'It is not my kind of spirituality. I am not the discipline kind of person. Why should my prayer time be another time for work?' Often this discouragement veils a recurrent feeling of failure and inadequacy, the weak side of our damaged and self-rejecting ego. 'I'm no good at anything – even meditation.'

What we need above all at this initial stage is an insight into the meaning of meditation and a thirst arising from a deeper level of consciousness from the one we seem stuck at. It is here right at the outset, therefore, that we encounter, although we may not yet recognise it as such, the prompting of grace. It comes from outside us in the form of teaching, tradition, spiritual friendship and inspiration. From within, it comes as the intuitive thirst for deeper experience. Christ, who as Spirit is no more within us than outside us, seems to push from outside and pull from within.

It helps to understand clearly from the beginning what is the meaning and purpose of the mantra. It is not a magic wand that blanks the mind or a switch that turns on God, but a discipline, 'beginning in faith and ending in love', which brings us into poverty of spirit. We do not say the mantra to fight off the distractions but to help us remove our attention from them. Simply discovering that we are, however poorly, free to place our attention elsewhere is the first great awakening. It is the beginning of the deepening of consciousness which allows us to leave the distractions on the surface, like waves on the surface of the ocean. Even at this earliest stage of the journey we are learning the profoundest truth, as we leave our religious as well as our ordinary thoughts behind: it is not our prayer but the prayer of Christ that concerns us. As the centre of consciousness shifts from the ego to the true self, all notion of 'my' and 'mine' begins to weaken.

As long as we are living anything like a normal life this level of consciousness will be the first one we meet each time we meditate. On bad days and in dark nights it may seem we have never gone beyond it. But merely to be aware of it and to face it is to begin to transcend it. Gradually a change does take place at this surface level. We notice it first perhaps in the ways we are more able to sit quietly without needing to read a magazine or take an old anxiety off the shelf, in patience and a sense of the presence of God in traffic jams or supermarket queues. A calmer and steadier mental life emerges in daily relationships. At meditation we become familiar, friends with, the patterns and habits of our mind and more tolerant of its wayward ways.

Second level

Reaching the second level, of zone, or consciousness does not mean we have forever mastered the discipline of the first level. We carry most of our faults with us all the way. At this next, deeper level we encounter the storage vaults of our lives. Everything we have done or said or thought or imagined, every impression, real or imagined, has its place here within the organic entity of our psyche. The great filing systems of this unique inner universe are our relationships, real and imagined, whatever has been done or said to us.

Here we must face what our unconscious processes have decided for us that we should not face. Lost, forgotten or buried memories with their attendant emotions and thoughts can be stirred up and released if they are blocking the movement of consciousness towards the true centre of personal identity. Sometimes this work of healing, integration and self-acceptance can be as turbulent in its way as the surface distractions. Strong emotions, such as anxiety, fear or anger can emerge from nowhere and for no apparent reason. More rarely, vivid memories of forgotten events are replayed on the inward eye of the imagination.

Usually, however, it is a work carried on below the surface of the conscious mind, out of the range of the ego's camera. The mantra then becomes like the seed in the parable of Jesus which a man planted in the earth while he went off and lived his daily life. All the time, the seed was growing in the dark womb of the earth, 'how, he did not know'.

If the danger at the first level is that we will become discouraged and turn back, there is another danger at this level. We may also find when the going gets tough at times that we demand some of the instant peace and consolation that we thought meditation promised us. But an equally grave danger is that we become fascinated with ourselves. The unconscious as it is penetrated by the light of consciousness has many strange and fascinating creatures to show us. There are many wonderful rooms to explore among the psyche's furnaces, workrooms, libraries and service centres. The faithful repetition of the mantra can seem rather uninteresting or distracting by contrast with these wonders. But fidelity at this stage has greater wonders to reveal than we can possibly imagine.

Self-knowledge, in the spiritual meaning of the term, is not restricted to what we discover about ourselves at this level of consciousness. But the full knowledge of the Self to which we are journeying is prepared for by what we pass through in this stage. It can be thought of both as purification and liberation and at times, when our deepest fears and shadows are uncovered, even as exorcism. From what happens at this level we become aware, at other times of reflection or prayer, of the major structures of our personality. We see the needs we had which life did not meet and the wounds which resulted. Wounds we hide or flaunt. Out of these wounds we can see the images of hope and happiness emerge which we then pursue down the highways and byways of life. We see the patterns in our relationships become visible and we can trace them back to ourselves rather than blame them only on others. We discover that we have become what we are because of how we have reacted and interacted (or refused to) rather than just from what was done to us.

Like all knowledge, this psychological self-awareness has equal potential for creativity or for destructiveness. It can spin a web of self-absorption and a shell of self-sufficiency. Or it can show us the power of forgiveness and tolerance from within the primary relationship with ourselves and so empower us to live more fully and generously with all others in the bond of compassion.

Which direction this level of consciousness sends us in is all-important for the rest of our journey. There is much solitude and at times true suffering at this level. Grace therefore gives us the love and balm necessary for our decision to persevere. 'He was among the wild beasts; and the angels waited on him' (Mark 1:13). Here above all we realise the relationship between meditation and community. As we become the person we are called to be we understand that to be a person is more than being an ego, an individual in isolation. To be a person is to be in relationship. And so we discover something we cannot yet fully understand about the nature of reality itself: that God cannot be impersonal.

The turbulence of this level of consciousness is variable. At times there are great calms: stretches where we feel we are integrated and that we have got it together. Then our behaviour one day or an inner swell of feeling from nowhere reminds us that this process will carry on for as long as we are making the journey. Similarly our surface distractions are there, perhaps unremarked, even as we are absorbed in deeper thoughts. A fuller, more mature psychological self begins to form. We recognise it as bearing our name and appearance. We can own it without shame or regret and with love. Yet this very act of recognition and acceptance proves that this is not the end of the journey. This self we can look at and think about we must also leave behind. Earlier we left the busy, surface, daily self running from one activity to the next. Yet with the opening of deeper levels we seem if anything busier than before. Life goes on at many levels simultaneously, all harmonising with each other through the faith and love of the mantra. With this greater inner harmony we are ready for another deepening.

Third level

The ego has been our constant companion from the beginning. Now at the third level we meet it head on. At the first level we met it in its most frazzled state, dressed in the ever-changing costumes of daily life. At the second stage it is dressed in the more dramatic period costumes of the different stages of our psychological history, acting out its many roles as victim, exploiter, child, adolescent, adult, religious seeker, rebel or conformist; trickster, griever, lover, magician, warrior, king or queen.

It is from the ego that all resistance to this journey to the true self arises. And yet the ego is the vehicle of the journey as well. Typically today we focus on the vehicle rather than the journey. Just as we make an idol out of the motor car which is no more than a useful means of transportation, we can focus so strongly on the ego and its processes that we lose sight of the spiritual meaning of the whole person.

At this third level of consciousness, however, we confront the ego in its naked existence, all the costumes temporarily laid aside. The *Cloud of Unknowing* describes this stage as a 'stark awareness of your own existence' subsisting between ourselves and God. This awareness, too, the *Cloud* tells us, must go before 'we can experience contemplation in its perfection'. It is an awareness touched by the deepest existential sorrow – not a sorrow about anything that has happened but at the fact of individual existence being inherently separate from Being. We must face and eventually transcend this existential sorrow before we can taste the joy of being.

Here too we understand the meaning of taking up our cross each day and following the Lord. Our cross is decorated by the trials of life but the wood of the cross is this naked sense of the separateness of the ego. No act of the will can lift us over this final hurdle, no technique can whisk it away. We are invited to sit at the foot of the cross at this stage in an ever purer faith. When waiting at a stoplight there is no alternative to patience. John Main remarked that more not less faith is needed as we pursue the pilgrimage. Here, where we face not merely distraction but the root and cause of distraction, our faith deepens and matures through the co-operation between our spirit and the Spirit of God until we are ready – the co-operation we see as synchronicity and call destiny.

The fidelity and maturity we have grown in during the earlier stages stands us in good stead at this level. Our friend the mantra has by now become rooted and the earlier doubts and compromises present in the early stages of any relationship have given way. The *Cloud* reminds us of the need to be faithful to the 'one little word' 'in peace and war', just as Cassian insisted we say the 'formula' 'in prosperity and adversity'. John Main's emphasis on simple fidelity to the mantra 'from the beginning to the end of each meditation' is in this ancient tradition of Christian prayer, practical, helpful, wise. It makes full sense, however, only as our own experience teaches us.

What happens next?

A cartoon of two zen meditators shows one asking this question of the other, who replies, 'What do you mean, what happens next, this is it!'

We have to be prepared for this being 'it' for a while. Yet faith is not just a matter of stubborn endurance. It is also a new way of vision. And as faith has grown so it has enabled us to see something of what is beyond physical or mental perception. We know we are not waiting without hope or joy. 'You have not seen him, yet you love him; and trusting in him now without seeing him, you are transported with a joy too great for words, while you reap the harvest of your faith, that is, salvation for your souls' (1 Peter 1:8–9). Gradually and suddenly the light of a lamp shining in a murky place, as St Peter describes it, gives way to daybreak and the morning star rises to illuminate our hearts and minds (2 Peter 1:19).

The ego's naked sense of its own finite existence is like a brick wall we cannot get over by ourselves. In God's time and by free gift an opening appears in that wall of selfhood. In that opening of self-transcendence we leave self behind and find our true self in Christ. So at this moment an encounter occurs with the humanity of Jesus unlike any other meeting or recognition that occurred at earlier stages. Here we meet him in the pure non-dual action of the Spirit, beyond any image or idea we might have of him. This occurs in the reality of the Spirit which underpins all dogma and doctrine. (We put our faith in the reality to which the words point, as Aquinas said, not in the words themselves.)

As John Main said of this stage of the journey, we meet Jesus at the frontier of our own identity and he becomes our guide into the new country of God, the kingdom. Everything Jesus said of himself makes sense through this encounter: door of the sheepfold, way, truth, life, resurrection, nourishing vine, friend.

Recognising him in this encounter is redemptive. It concentrates our being in so fully personal and unique an experience of love that it becomes the standard of Truth by which all other experiences or insights must be judged. Here at this opening in ourselves and beyond ourselves we are illumined by the Spirit to make the journey with Jesus, in the mind of Christ, into the boundless love of God.

When will this happen? In a sense, because of the Incarnation and Resurrection it has already happened in each of us. It is only a reality waiting to be awakened to. Physics has discovered the dual nature of matter as being both wave and particle, depending upon our way of looking at it. In the same way our pilgrimage of meditation through these different levels of consciousness can be seen as either successive – one stage following the other – or simultaneous – it is all now. Both are true, depending on the way we look at it. The way we see is decided by the depth of vision faith has clarified for us.

In that vision we can look forwards and backwards from the still point of the present moment. We can see how every stage of our journey, even the superficial levels of the distracted monkey mind, have been touched and guided all along by the Spirit who is now revealing Jesus to us, removing the veil. We now see how the deeper conflicts and wounds of our psyche at the second level are shot through with the healing power of the Spirit. And, as we see how every part of us lives and moves in God, the fruits of the Spirit begin to manifest themselves at all the levels of our existence.

Meditation is a way of faith and of love. By passing through its stages we learn that faith is more than belief. 'Even the devil believes in God.' Too much emphasis on dogmatic orthodoxy therefore actually reduces faith. Faith is essentially the personal commitment to relationship – so we talk about faithful marriages and friends. Faith is developed only through time, yet its growth reveals a union of love which is stronger than death, the lord of time.

If meditation changes our life it is not through magic but in faith. The mantra becomes a sacrament of faith – a sacrament of relationship and union. By learning to be faithful in small things, such as the saying of the word, we learn to be faithful in all the relationships of life. It is, as Jesus said, a narrow road, but it expands beyond the zero point of letting go into the infinite expansion of being we are called to in God.

The journey is never dull if we make it in faith. The stillness is never static. And over it all, the open-armed, all-accepting embrace of Christ presides. He is the gate, the goal and the whole way. Our lives are soaked in Christ. There is nowhere he is not.

With much love

Laurence

Laurence Freeman OSB

The World Community for Christian Meditation

Meditation creates community. Since the first Christian Meditation Centre was started by John Main in 1975 a steadily growing Community of Christian meditators has spread around the world. Individual meditators frequently begin to meet in small weekly groups and the network of these groups provides wider support and encouragement for people who wish to sustain their daily practice of morning and evening meditation.

The groups meet in homes, parishes, schools, prisons, businesses, communities and government departments. Beginning with a short teaching on meditation, often drawn from the Community's collection of taped talks by John Main, the group then meditates together in silence for half an hour. After this there is time for discussion. The groups are by nature ecumenical and practise an open-door hospitality, welcoming anyone who comes sincerely seeking silence.

About twenty-five Christian Meditation Centres, some residential, others in meditators' homes, also serve to communicate the way of silence taught in this tradition. The Centres help co-ordinate the local groups and welcome people seeking a deeper spiritual path from whatever direction they may be coming.

A quarterly newsletter giving spiritual teaching and reflection is sent out from London and distributed from a number of national Centres together with local and international news of retreats, and other events being held in the Community.

An annual John Main Seminar is held, usually in Europe and North America in alternate years. Previous leaders of the Seminar, which is a three-day symposium with meditation and reflection, have included Bede Griffiths, Jean Vanier, William Johnston, the Dalai Lama, Laurence Freeman and Raimon Panikkar.

The Community is served from an International Centre based in London which co-ordinates the Newsletter, the John Main Seminar and new publications as well as responding to the spiritual search and questions of many inquirers from around the world. This Centre is funded entirely by donations and especially through a Friends of the International Centre program by which individuals or groups commit to giving £50.00 or $100.00, or equivalent in local currency, direct to the Centre. If you would like to become a Friend please write to 'Friends Program', International Centre, The World Community for Christian Meditation, 23 Kensington Square, London W8 5HN, UK (Fax: 0171 937 6790).

If you would like to contact a local Christian Meditation Group near you, you can contact one of the Centres listed on pp. 152–4 or write direct to the International Centre in London.

Chronicle 1982–1995

To 1982

The story of the World Community for Christian Meditation could be said to have begun the day in 1951 when John Main, then an aide to the Governor of Malaya, paid a courtesy call on an Indian monk living on the outskirts of Kuala Lumpur, Swami Sattyananda (1909–1963). The purpose of the visit was to thank the monk for his contribution to the social harmony of the different races and creeds of the country, but in the course of their conversation John Main realised he was in the presence of a spiritual teacher who was to change the course of his life. The monk introduced John Main to the simple practice of meditation, morning and evening, with the discipline of the mantra. He was still integrating this practice into his regular life of Christian prayer when he returned to Europe to become a professor of law.

In 1958 John Main entered a Benedictine monastery in London and to his dismay was instructed to give up his meditation practice because it was not part of the Christian tradition. It was the beginning, he said, of a period of spiritual desert. But after profession and ordination and at the busiest period of his monastic life, while he was headmaster of a Bendictine school in the United States, he began a study of the spiritual teachings on prayer by the early Christian monks of the fourth century. In the *Conferences* of John Cassian John Main found the Christian teaching on the mantra, the faithful repetition of a single word or phrase by which the mind detaches itself from thought and comes to silence and stillness.

Restored to his path of meditation, John Main went on to teach it from the Christian tradition, enriched by his Christian theology and life of prayer, to people of all walks of life. When he died in 1982 the first signs were already evident that his work was bearing fruit in a world-wide, ecumenical Community of Christians realising the deeper dimensions of their faith through a contemplative discipline of daily meditation.

One of the important ways in which this Community began was through the newsletter which John Main began to send out to meditators from 1977, the year he started his small Benedictine monastic and lay community in Canada. The first twelve of these were collected and published as *Letters from the Heart* (New York: Crossroad, 1980), and this was followed by a second collection entitled *The Present Christ* (Darton, Longman and Todd, 1985). These letters combined news of the local and the growing international Community with a substantial teaching on the spiritual meaning of meditation.

1982–1991

Laurence Freeman, his friend and disciple, succeeded John Main after his death and helped direct a period of considerable growth of the teaching of Christian meditation around the world. In 1985 the first series of teachings were held in Australia where an extensive community and network of groups has formed. With the encouragment of Fr Bede Griffiths, Fr Laurence first visited India in 1988, where a Christian Meditation Centre was opened in Calicut. A similar pattern was repeated in Singapore, Thailand and Malaysia, where teaching visits led to the formation of small weekly groups and a co-ordinating Centre. An annual John Main Seminar began in 1983. In 1990 the Canadian community was closed because of the difficulties involved in combining an international meditation centre with a house of monastic formation. The International Centre returned to London where a Meditation Centre had been opened in Kensington in 1985. Fr Laurence joined the Monastery of Christ the King, Cockfosters, a Benedictine monastery in the Olivetan Congregation with which the World Community enjoys a special relationship.

In 1991 the John Main Seminar was led in New Harmony, Indiana, by Bede Griffiths, who spoke on John Main's teaching and influence, talks which were published as *The New Creation in Christ* (Darton, Longman and Todd, 1992). During this Seminar meditators from around the world agreed to form the World Community for Christian Meditation with an International Centre to serve the teaching of meditation and co-ordinate the quarterly newsletter and the John Main Seminar. At the same time a publishing company, Medio Media, was created to ensure the availability of John Main's works and to encourage a contemporary spiritual literature rooted in the Christian contemplative tradition and in dialogue with other faiths and the modern world.

From 1977 a number of meditators had taken the step of becoming Benedictine Oblates, lay members of a monastic family, this action springing out of the shared commitment to meditation in this tradition. This Oblate community continues to evolve around the world in affiliation with the Olivetan Congregation. One of these, a Canadian, Paul Harris, has dedicated himself full-time to the work of the Community and travels extensively encouraging groups and introducing meditation. In Singapore Peter and Patricia Ng lead the Centre and network of groups, an example of the many couples who form part of the Community and its work world-wide. In London Giovanni Felicioni directs the Community's publishing company, Medio Media Ltd.

1992–1995

This is the period of the Community's life covered by this present collection of newsletters. A summary of the main events of this time was given in each of the quarterly letters.

Letter One (February 1992)

A magazine commemorating John Main's tenth anniversary with articles representing the global community of meditators was issued. Laurence Freeman with members of the Indian and UK Centres gave a series of talks and retreats around India.

Letter Two (May 1992)

Laurence Freeman spent a week at Bede Griffiths' ashram of Shantivanam. He also visited the Singapore Centre and gave teachings there. The International Directory of meditation groups was produced by the Singapore Centre. The International Centre reported on news of groups forming in Zambia.

Bede Griffiths visited the International Centre in London and taught there and at the monastery in Cockfosters. A new Centre was opened in Brussels. After Easter Laurence Freeman visited Washington DC and Florida for retreats and talks. He also spoke in Ottawa, Toronto, Montreal and British Columbia. A Korean translation of John Main's first book, *The Gethsemani Talks*, was made. A video interview with Bede Griffiths, *Christ in the Lotus*, was published by Medio Media.

Letter Three (September 1992)

Jean Vanier led the ninth John Main Seminar ('From Brokenness to Wholeness: Following Jesus') in London. The first Monte Oliveto meditation retreat was held after the Seminar at the mother monastery of the Olivetan Congregation near Siena. Laurence Freeman led retreats in Ireland.

Letter Four (March 1993)

December 30, John Main's anniversary, was as usual kept as a day of silence at the London Centre. Fr Bede suffered a serious stroke on December 20. A Conference on 'Asian Contemplative Christianity' was held in Manila, organised by the Christian Meditation Centre of the Philippines. Speakers included Fr William Johnston SJ, Vandana Mataji RCSJ and Laurence Freeman OSB. Paul Harris taught in England and Ireland, Peter Ng introduced meditation in the RCIA programme in Singapore. Fr Laurence taught in Belgium. Ria Weyens, a Belgian member of the London community, visited Belgium regularly for talks organised by Agnes D'Hooghe of the Brussels Centre. A Polish monk, Jan Bereza, began teaching Christian meditation and translating John Main in Poland.

Letter Five (June 1993)

Fr Bede died on May 13 at Shantivanam. A Memorial Mass was celebrated at Westminster Cathedral, London on June 15.

Laurence Freeman spoke in Florida and at Princeton and Harvard Universities and in New York. A Centre opened at the Monastery of Christ the King, Cockfosters. John Cotling, a Manchester meditator, opened his home as a Centre. The UK Trust Council was formed to serve the teaching of meditation in this country. Sr Madeline Simon, first director of the London Centre, retired. Paul Harris spent several weeks teaching in Ireland. Laurence Freeman gave retreats in Canada and the Philippines. John Main's *Word Made Flesh* was published, Paul Harris' *Meditation by Those Who Practice It*, and Madeleine Simon's book on meditation for children, *Born Contemplative*.

Letter Six (September 1993)

William Johnston SJ led the John Main Seminar in Toronto on 'The New Mysticism'. A retreat at Niagara followed the Seminar. The Monte Oliveto retreat was held in June with Robert Kiely and Giovanni Felicioni helping to lead it. William Johnston visited the London Centre and spoke at Cockfosters. An interim Constitution for the World Community for Christian Meditation was adopted in Toronto. Sr Margaret Collier, director of the Cork Centre, organised a retreat led by Laurence Freeman. The Australian National Forum was held in Melbourne, co-ordinated by John Little. Elizabeth West of the London Centre led Buddhist–Christian retreats. Eileen Byrne, director of the London Centre, continued to co-ordinate plans for a national conference of Christian meditators. Milo Coerper, chairperson of the John Main Institute in the USA, Sr Eileen O'Hea CSJ and Laurence Freeman met with Fr Thomas Keating in the context of a Benedictine experience week in New Harmony, Indiana. Dominic Schofield began a project within the Community to explore the relationship between social and spiritual values in South-East Asia.

Letter Seven (December 1993)

Laurence Freeman and others visited India where retreats were held in several cities and a meeting took place with Mother Teresa. A Memorial Mass at Westminster Cathedral was held for John Todd who led the 1987 John Main Seminar and who died in June. Michelle Dubuc in Montreal developed the French Meditation Centre there. Paul Harris travelled to Asia, Britain and Ireland. In Florida the national US retreat was organised by Pat and Chuck Prescott. Benita Lankford, the California co-ordinator, arranged a retreat led by Laurence Freeman at San Luis Rey. He also spoke in San Diego. A conference on Filipino spirituality was held in Manila. Laurence Freeman spoke at other places in the Philippines, Singapore and Ireland.

Letter Eight (June 1994)

Giovanni Felicioni led days on meditation and yoga in London where he teaches yoga. Sr Evelyn McDevitt began to form Christian Meditation groups in Belfast. The UK Group Leaders' Conference was recognised as a milestone in the sense of community and depth among the meditators. Laurence Freeman visited Thailand, Malaysia and Singapore and later in this period went to lead a retreat in the Yukon where the most northerly groups in the Community have formed. Paul Harris taught in Belfast, other parts of Ireland and the UK.

Letter Nine (October 1994)

His Holiness the Dalai Lama led the 1994 John Main Seminar, 'The Good Heart', in London in September. Four hundred participants of different faiths heard him comment on the Gospels, meditated with him three times a day and shared the dialogue he entered with panels drawn from meditators in the Community. Mark Schofield, consultant to Medio Media, helped co-ordinate recording of the Seminar which was filmed and later produced as a video. Professor Robert Kiely of Harvard University was elected Chairperson of the Guiding Board of the Community. A 'Monk Within' experience was held at Monte Oliveto for a dozen young men after the annual retreat. Laurence Freeman taught in Italy, Ireland and Belgium.

Letter Ten (December 1994)

The Good Heart videos of the Dalai Lama Seminar were published by Medio Media and began to be shown widely at Centres and interfaith meetings. Laurence Freeman led retreats in Canada, California and Ireland. Groups began in Malta and Fiji. The Centre in New Zealand was relaunched. A team from the International Centre spent three weeks teaching in India on a visit organised by Rose Isaac and Dr Jo Velacherry of the Calicut Centre.

Letter Eleven (March 1995)

The 'Communitas' tapes – talks on meditation by John Main which have inspired meditators world-wide for many years – were re-issued as a subscription series. The Guiding Board meeting at Harvard discussed the Community's financial situation and agreed to a number of ways of informing meditators of the urgent need for support if the International Centre is to continue its work. Laurence Freeman visited Singapore and Malaysia; he gave a weekend in Dublin for 500 people organised by Monsignor Tom Fehily, director of the Dublin Meditation Centre; he also led a retreat in Portugal and a day for the bishop and clergy of the diocese of Palm Beach, Florida, before going to New York where he spoke to a newly formed Christian Meditation group in the Dag Hammarskjöld Meditation Room at the United Nations in New York. Paul Harris led a series of seminars and day workshops on meditation around Canada.

Letter Twelve (June 1995)

Laurence Freeman visited Brazil for the first time for a series of retreats and talks introducing Christian meditation, arranged by Brazilian meditators. Sr Maria Emanuel OSB, Thomas Merton's Portuguese translator, had prepared the way by her translation of John Main. Sergio de Morais, the director of the Centre in Rio de Janeiro, co-ordinated the visit, during which Laurence Freeman also met Dom Helder Camara in Recife. The 'Friends of the International Centre' programme was launched to enable meditators around the world to contribute to the work of the Community by means of an annual donation of £50/$100 direct to the Centre. The new video by Medio Media, *Coming Home*, introducing meditation, was released. Paul Harris spoke in several locations in Ireland. Laurence Freeman visited Belfast. William Johnston spoke in Australia on a tour organised by the Christian Meditation Community as part of its celebration of its tenth anniversary. Arrangements were in preparation for the 1995 John Main Seminar 'On Jesus' to be led by Laurence Freeman in San Diego.

Christian Meditation on the Internet

- WCCM.ARCHIVES:
  ftp://byrd.mu.wvnet.edu/pub/merton/wccm
  http://www.marshall.edu/~/stepp/vri/merton/WCCM.html

- WCCM.FORUM:
  Send email to LISTSERV@WVNVM.WVNET.EDU with the following lines of text SUBSCRIBE MERTON-L YOUR NAME (substituting your real name for YOUR NAME) SET MERTON-L TOPICS:+T6

Medio Media

Medio Media is the publishing arm of The World Community for Christian Meditation. It is committed to the dissemination of the teaching of meditation in the Christian tradition, and in particular to the work of John Main. It is also committed to furthering the growing dialogue among meditators and seekers from all traditions based on the deeper experience of silence shared among all religions.

A catalogue of Medio Media including books, audio cassettes and videos, representing, among other authors, John Main, Bede Griffiths, Laurence Freeman, William Johnston and the Dalai Lama is available free from:

Medio Media
23 Kensington Square
London W8 5HN
UK
Tel: 0171 937 4679
Fax: 0171 937 6790

Christian Meditation Centres

International Centre
23 Kensington Square
London W8 5HN
Tel: 0171 937 4679
Fax: 0171 937 6790

Australia
Christian Meditation Network
PO Box 6630
St Kilda Road
Melbourne, Vic. 3004
Tel: 03 989 4824
Fax: 03 525 4917

Christian Meditation Centre
PO Box 323
Tuart Hill, WA 6060
Tel/Fax: 9 444 5810

Belgium
Christelijk Meditatie Centrum
Beiaardlaan 1
1850 Grimbergen
Tel: 02 269 5071

Brazil
Nucleo Dom John Main
CP 33266
CEP 22442–970
Rio de Janeiro RJ
Fax: 21 322 4171

Canada
Meditatio
PO Box 552, Station NDG
Montreal, Quebec H4A 3P9
Tel: 514 766 0475
Fax: 514 937 8178

John Main Centre
470 Laurier Avenue, Apt 708
Ottawa, Ontario K1R 7W9
Tel: 613 236 9437
Fax: 613 236 2821

Christian Meditation Centre
10 Maple St
Dartmouth, N.S. B2Y 2X3
Tel: 902 466 6691

India
Christian Meditation Centre
1/1429 Bilathikulam Road
Calicut
673006 Kerala
Tel: 495 60395

Ireland
Christian Meditation Centre
4 Eblana Avenue
Dun Laoghaire, Co Dublin
Tel: 01 2801505

Christian Meditation Centre
58 Meadow Grove
Blackrock, Cork
Tel: 021 357249

New Zealand
Christian Meditation Centre

PO Box 35531
Auckland 1310
Tel: 64 9 478 3438
Fax: 64 9 478 6367

Philippines
Christian Meditation Centre
5/f Chroncile Bldg, Cor. Tektite
   Road
Meralco Avenue/Pasig
M. Manila
Tel: 02 633 3364
Fax: 02 631 3104

Singapore
Christian Meditation Centre
9 Mayfield Street
Singapore 438 023
Tel: 65 348 6790

Thailand
Christian Meditation Centre
51/1 Sedsiri Road
Bangkok 10400
Tel: 271 3295

United Kingdom
Christian Meditation Centre
29 Campden Hill Road
London W8 7DX
Tel/Fax: 0171 912 1371

Christian Meditation Centre
13 Langdale Road
Sale, Cheshire M33 4EW
Tel: 0161 976 2577

Christian Meditation Centre
Monastery of Christ the King
Bramley Road
London N14 4HE

Tel: 0181 449 6648
Fax: 0181 449 2338

Christian Meditation Centre
29 Mansion House Road
Glasgow
Scotland G41 3DN
Tel: 0141 649 4448

United States
John Main Institute
7315 Brookville Road
Chevy Chase, MD 20815
Tel: 301 652 8635

Christian Meditation Centre
1080 West Irving Park Road
Roselle, IL 60172
Tel/Fax: 708 351 2613

Christian Meditation Centre
322 East 94th Street No 4B
New York, NY 10128
Tel: 212 831 5710

Christian Meditation Centre
1101 S. Arlington Ave
Los Angeles, CA 90019
Tel: 213 732 8615

Christian Meditation Centre
2490 18th Avenue
Kingsburg, CA 93631
Tel: 209 897 3711

Hesed Community
3745 Elston Avenue
Oakland, CA 94602
Tel: 415 482 5573

Christian Meditation Centre
1619 Wight Street
Wall, NJ 07719
Tel: 908 681 6238
Fax: 908 280 5999